T0339419

"It is highly refreshing to read a book on leadership about cautionary tales. The twenty vignettes gathered over many years of the authors' management and consulting experience, combined with the seven leadership attributes to avoid such failures, have important lessons for anyone who wants to shine as a leader."

Shantha Mohan, *Mentor, Carnegie Mellon Integrated Innovation Institute; Author of* Leadership Lessons with The Beatles: Actionable Tips and Tools for Becoming Better at Leading.

"Far too often, we share stories around the proverbial fire of what worked in our leadership journeys. But what lessons are missed when we can't linger with the times where our grand ambitions failed to come to fruition? In this book, the authors do a masterful job walking through their own leadership journeys at the point of failure, using those moments to cast a light for all of us in our own work."

Peter Boumgarden, *Koch Professor of Practice for Family Enterprise, Washington University in St. Louis*

"Having spent 30+ years in the government in senior level positions, retiring as Deputy Assistant Secretary of Defense, and 12+ years in the private sector, this book on Leadership Failures is a must read to avoid the frequent mistakes all of us have made or witnessed in our careers. The book format creates an easy-to-visualize roadmap to facilitate self-reflection. I was most impressed with the inspiring quotes, vignettes about failures, and attributes for success to help you move forward."

Robert F. Lentz, *former Deputy Assistant Secretary of Defense and CEO Cyber Security Strategies*

"Brilliant. Simply brilliant. If you are tired of sports coaches touting leadership principles of generals, generals touting leadership principles of corporate CEOs, and corporate CEOs using sports metaphors and touting the great leadership of coaches, you need to read a book that is truly helpful, not hackneyed. *Leadership Failures* is that book. Failure is a far better teacher than fortuitous success – the lessons learned from failure are seared into our minds. Told with humor, pathos, and rock-solid analysis, *Leadership Failures* is the best guide I know of to lead you to leadership success."

Joseph L. Shaefer, *Brigadier General, USAF, Retired*

Leadership Failures

Humans make mistakes. Many of us lose career ascendency or risk destroying our institutions by doubling down on or ignoring outcomes of our own poor decisions.

Good leaders learn and teach from their errors. Professions are strengthened. Institutions thrive. Careers grow.

Through real-life stories that focus on senior/board leadership from multiple walks of life, and brief discussions of significant attributes, readers will be challenged to diagnose and turn missteps into positive growth experiences.

The authors of this book have had extensive careers in public and private, for-profit and not-for-profit settings, and in independent and government-sponsored consulting, development, academic, and clinical environments. Without having any single leadership paradigm to push, they raise questions about outcomes for institutions that are affected and individual career paths.

Their cautionary tales ask readers to think through "next steps" or prevent the need to get there; hence, this is an ideal extra-assignment book in graduate management courses and for managers seeking to work their way up toward higher leadership roles. Board members also can learn from its non-industry-specific target readership.

Leadership Failures

Precautionary Tales and Prevention Strategies

Kate M. Fenner • Mark W. Reifsteck • Peter Fenner

Routledge
Taylor & Francis Group

A PRODUCTIVITY PRESS BOOK

First published 2023
by Routledge
605 Third Avenue, New York, NY 10158

and by Routledge
2 Park Square, Milton Park, Abingdon, Oxon, OX14 4RN

Routledge is an imprint of the Taylor & Francis Group, an informa business

ISBN: 9781032303031 (hbk)
ISBN: 9781032302997 (pbk)
ISBN: 9781003304371 (ebk)

DOI: 10.4324/9781003304371

Typeset in Garamond
by Deanta Global Publishing Services, Chennai, India

To those who tried, failed, and tried again.
We have learned a lot from you.

Contents

Preface

Three Envelopes: An Important Opening Parable

> You can't coach height
>   – A basketball metaphor meaning that you
>   should go with your strengths

This is an old, worn parable of leadership. If you've heard it multiple times, it is only because it is such an apt metaphor describing the arc of a senior leader's tenure in many organizations. We have heard, seen, and participated in organizations where the three-envelope parable was applicable. Please read knowing the validity of the underlying principle: Everything is temporary.

A new CEO enters her office on the first day. Opening the desk drawer, she finds three envelopes clipped together with a brief cover note from her predecessor stating, "Open one envelope whenever you are in an impossible situation that appears career ending." She smiles, places the envelopes aside, and launches into her new role with enthusiasm.

Inevitably, a huge and seemingly intractable problem arises with devastating outcomes. She racks her brain attempting to deduce a possible solution. Finally, she recalls the envelopes and opens the one marked "#1." It states, "Blame me for whatever occurred." She follows the instructions, giving her Board the explanation for failure as residing with the previous CEO, and life resumes apace.

Sometime later, a second crisis with a miserable outcome occurs. Once again, she selects an envelope, this time, marked "#2," opens it and reads "Hire and blame a consultant." She proceeds as instructed, after which life returns to normal and moves on.

Following a peaceful period, a third seemingly intractable crisis hits. In need again, she opens the envelope marked "#3." Inside is a simple statement – "Prepare three envelopes."

The parable is amusing, and to experienced leaders a bit too familiar. The core message is to understand that regardless of time spent in the role, all leadership positions are temporary; there is no permanence to the vast majority of senior roles even if one has been successful for years. In fact, long tenure frequently is too long: It can mean that there isn't continuous development of new knowledge and skills.

Often a long tenure indicates risk aversion, stagnation, and a tendency to "play it safe." If this security-seeking, long-tenured person is in a critical senior position, the organization can suffer from strategic stasis – not changing to meet the demands of the marketplace or to take advantage of emerging technology.

We have lived this three-envelope parable, sometimes without even recognizing that the process was in play. We are without any purpose in this book beyond sharing a bit of hard-earned wisdom and hoping the stories entertain and educate. We have also watched this process and advised others on how to cope with each stage. Sometimes you receive more than three chances at leadership crisis resolution, often not. Sometimes a leader can surmount a crisis without opening an envelope, but often the parable applies.

Our leadership journeys are complete, we have no more mountains to climb and no services to sell, so here and now we can be candid, without agenda except perhaps to enlighten a bit. We share a sampling of leadership crises that led to the final envelope for many folks, and hope also to share meaningful advice about how to meet and surmount each crisis.

Readers should note that we have chosen to focus on leadership failure – in fact, frequently spectacular incidents of failure that usually led to organizational expulsion whether by choice or by directive. Our focus on failures, as opposed to examples and examination of successes, is founded on several reasons.

First and foremost, there are multiple excellent, research-based tomes dedicated to leadership success, from Peters and Waterman, to Collins, and to Covey. They and other great minds have analyzed success and delineated reasons and principles for readers to consider. This is well-plowed ground and did not merit our meager abilities for attention.

Secondly, failures are as instructional and informative as successes, and abundantly more present. We have spent decades as consultants helping organizations and individual leaders cope with the detritus of failure: We have ample material for commentary. We also were able to extract useful lessons for future application and failure prevention which we share here.

Finally, failure observed but not experienced can be mildly entertaining, much like watching the dapper dandy slip on a banana peel: Observing the hubris that frequently precedes a fall can provide some sense of divine justice however fleeting.

Is This Book for You? Essential Elements

> Failures can be midwives to the birth of successful leadership
> – Anonymous

This book is intended to serve as a cautionary story. No one starts a leadership career by saying: ". . .hoping to develop a destructive leadership style." Poor leaders don't just suddenly emerge: They develop over time.

Leaders rarely exhibit a sudden devolution to incompetence. Frequently, small errors, lapses, and misjudgments signal the beginning of a slide toward incompetence. A small "white lie" allows the leader to cover a lapse in decision-making. He or she succeeds in that instance and learns to manipulate the truth to cope with difficult situations. Soon, being less than truthful becomes a pattern until the inevitable usually occurs: Reality has caught up with the need for candor, and manipulating the truth no longer works.

The vignettes we've included illustrate the culmination of an evolution in behavior – whether by instinct, inner deficits, or simply expeditious response to external pressure. Through deficits in personality, competence, or just learning that there is an easier path, poor leadership builds over time and doesn't emerge whole cloth.

Though perhaps difficult to self-assess, one can examine one's own leadership style to detect attributes of strength and potential vulnerabilities that lead toward leadership deficits. We ask the reader to approach this text with an attitude of introspection. What can be gleaned from these leadership fails that can be used to inform your leadership development?

Our experience in leading and consulting to complex organizations informs this book. We have not engaged in a series of empirical research projects for this work, but have retrospectively analyzed a multitude of cases, assignments, and crises to arrive at an experientially based paradigm of successful leadership.

Analysis of this experiential base reveals seven common and critical attributes that cut across all successful leaderships. These are introduced here for context and are explored more thoroughly for definition later. These attributes include the following:

1. *Honesty/integrity*: Truth-telling is critical, particularly when talking to yourself.
2. *Self-awareness*: Know thyself, and the rest will be easier.
3. *Emotional maturity*: Children, whether large or small, shouldn't occupy leadership roles.
4. *Communicator*: If you can't convey your message, then your effectiveness is also muted.
5. *Decisiveness*: The road to hell is paved in indecision.
6. *Intelligence*: Though contemporary politics might seem to indicate that any fool with a megaphone can succeed, leaders should be able to think critically, analyze, and make decisions on as much empirical evidence as is available. Learning is elemental to leadership, and intelligence drives these learnings into desired paths.
7. *Resilience*: Being able to get up again and return to the fray even after a knockdown blow.

Rarely (never in our experience) does one encounter a leader who possesses all seven critical attributes in depth. Everyone has strengths and limitations. Moreover, even if you possess several attributes in abundance, say intelligence and integrity, rarely will those attributes be present in equal amounts in multiple situations. Attribute strengths wax and wane, pushing forward on some occasions and diminishing in presence at other, perhaps critical, times. It is imperative to have a realistic perspective on which attributes you have in abundance, which are adequate, and where your limitations are; then, you can better pay attention to developmental needs and when it is best to rely upon the strengths of others.

Good leaders build teams; complex organizations rarely achieve any lasting goals on the efforts of one "hero." You do encounter the rare situation where someone saved the day, invented the key process for success, bagged the big account, or pioneered the market-moving product. This is quite rare, seldom serially replicable, and upon examination reveals that others contributed mightily to the achievement. Effective organizations are run by a constellation of people with different skill sets, abilities, and contributions.

Building an effective team is a key attribute of excellent leaders. Frequently, we are attracted to folks like ourselves, people with our attributes, attitudes, and decision-making style. Though understandably comfortable, this can be a fatal leadership flaw. Building from and toward a diversity of attributes, thinking styles, perspectives, and experience is a base to an effective team. A baseball team composed solely of skilled catchers would not win often. Neither does a team of homogeneous thinkers with similar preparation and experience. Smart leaders seek to balance their own strengths and weaknesses when recruiting colleagues to assure a multitude of perspectives for input. Of course, the leader must be receptive to such critical inputs.

If you are exceptionally strong at communication, able to convey thoughts, and ably convince folks to follow, that's a great skill. You don't need to build a team of colleagues with similar skills. But it is imperative to have colleagues with complementary skills, balancing your deficits and not merely reinforcing your assets.

For example, perhaps financial management is not your strength. That suggests recruiting talent with great financial analytical skills. Build a team thinking of a balanced set of critical attributes, perhaps overlapping but able to compensate for each other's limitations and depend on each other's strengths. Diversity is a deservedly well-regarded value for organizational leadership. We need to reach beyond our comfort zones to recruit and listen to people of different backgrounds, races, genders, and abilities.

The three of us have spent decades in organizations as Managers, Directors, Deans, VPs, and CEOs. Later, we have logged millions of air miles and years of service advising organizations from Universities to Health Systems, publicly held companies to closely owned investment houses. Along this path, we have had the privilege of working for, and with, many exemplary leaders – people who were able to bring the best out of their teams, accomplish remarkable success, and achieve stature and recognition in return for their incredible work.

We have also witnessed many organizational problems, tragedies, and farcical outcomes as leaders mismanaged, miscommunicated, and generally missed everything. We have been engaged to help steer organizational turnarounds, provide interim leadership to remedy incredible messes, support redesign, and encourage renewal after devastating decision implementation. We have been part of remarkable organizational rebirth after phenomenal leadership failures or simple malpractice. Each engagement, initiative, and interim role permitted us the opportunity not only to assist but also to learn. Some of our experiences were gained during organizational positions where we were able to witness and occasionally be the victim of truly inept leaders. Later we served as consultants frequently engaged to "bat in cleanup roles" or support significant change initiatives. We gained insight, learned what not to do in the face of emergency, and most of all had the privilege of working with scores of truly talented, wise, and ethical leaders.

There are many excellent tomes on the essence of leadership. This book is pointed in a different direction. Our aim is to tell cautionary tales, outline disasters great and small, and perhaps indicate the path to avoid. There are entertaining stories to be told along the way, some humorous, some with tragic outcomes for individuals and organizations. We have seen great organizations corrupted by greed, led to the brink of closure by ineptness, and revivified by new leadership.

We present cautionary tales for consideration and information. The reader is invited to read on two levels or perhaps with two goals in mind: One is interest and entertainment; the other is an opportunity for self-evaluation. Good stories about failure that are read and not experienced are interesting. But applying those same stories to one's own life can be instructional. Reading about how someone else touched the hot stove allows one to learn to avoid that pain without the actual experience. Errors are part of learning, why not avoid some by viewing others' pratfalls?

We also ask the reader to walk a mile in the shoes of the leaders herein described and the teams that experience the impact of failed leaders. Again, this text should entertain and educate. But to accomplish the latter, you as a reader will need to engage in a bit of introspection as you join the tales of "leadership fails."

The question "Could this ever be me?" is a first step in learning to avoid these pitfalls. You will read repeatedly that we focus on experience and episodic failures, rather than intending to set a single model for success or for failure. The bibliography can lead you to several examples of models for success by cited authors.

Many of the leaders reflected here can serve as role models of what *not* to do. Faculty frequently refer to the opportunity for a "negative teach," letting students experience an unhappy outcome as a way of learning. This book contains many examples that can serve as negative teaching moments, with the included stories depicting flawed decision-making, character, or judgment. The reader is invited, with the addition of a bit of our experience-based commentary, to use these stories to help shape future behaviors, as cautions of pitfalls to avoid, and habits of mind to eschew.

We hope that you'll agree that while there is entertainment here, there is also useful learning.

Prevention and Damage Control

> You cannot make this stuff up!

Many of the tales we tell here are entertaining … if it doesn't happen to you! The amount of abject stupidity and complete lack of insight that occurs can seem amazing, fictional even. Yet, we assure that these episodes are not only real but have happened (and like events are happening now) multiple times in the course of organizational life. Fantastical, ridiculous, and just plain stupid are apt descriptors of many of the events here told. Yet these leadership failures are encountered all too frequently in the trajectory of a career. Our intent is to record the failures we have witnessed, participated in, and cleaned up after, and to give a forewarning on avoiding, coping, or escaping such situations. But first, let us differentiate management and leadership to better understand the impact of leadership failure.

John Kotter, an éminence grise of leadership theory, clarifies management as the functions that make a system work, while leadership builds or transforms the system. Think of managers as occupying a box of responsibility with defined boundaries, known limits, and clear expectations. The manager succeeds by performing acceptably within the box. Leaders push the boundaries, expand the box, and build new boxes or functions for organizations.

Many folks who function well for decades within the management role are never tempted to exceed the box in which they work. This is fine! Knowing your goals, preferences, and limitations, and choosing to stay within that framework is admirable. Not everyone should be "moving up" as an ambition. Family, community, and outside personal interest may all create the need to stay within a circumscribed role. It is admirable to know one's priorities and respond according to same.

People focused on leadership, however, tend to examine boundaries for opportunities to exceed same, look for new, better, and different experiences. Great leaders do not necessarily spring from good managers, though frequently first having a manager role is the path to a leadership role. Leadership is not an innate trait that simply emerges when the situation demands same. Though there are abilities and talents that favor leadership emerging, say being more extroverted or having a disciplined attitude toward work, these don't comprise a leader. Just as one learns any discipline, one learns leadership.

Know that good managers frequently cannot succeed as leaders; the absence of boundaries, rules, and regulations can create untenable tension. Too often good managers are promoted with an expectation of evolving to higher leadership roles, then fail simply not only because the expectation is beyond their preparation or ken, but also because those expectations were never clearly defined by supervisors above them.

Moreover, finding a good leader often reveals much "time in grade" – a succession of increasingly more responsible roles that build leadership capabilities one layer or attribute upon another. Leadership is acquired through practice, development, experience, and, if one is fortunate, good mentorship. Having a title doesn't confer a leadership ability; many folks designated as formal leaders in organizations are miserably prepared for the role and then fail, too many publicly and spectacularly.

Leadership failures tend to produce a cascade of organizational impacts – the detritus of failure. When a leader fails spectacularly, the failure impacts many other parts of the organization. Like a stone thrown into a calm pool, the ripples play out across the company. The higher the leader's role, the greater the impact.

We have seen complete organizational collapse after CEO failure. We've participated in organizational rescue from "Near Death Experience" (public story memorialized while in a consulting role*). The human toll of leadership failure extends far beyond the impact on the person involved. It not only scars the leader but can hobble the entire enterprise.

Part of the purpose of this book is to give the reader a forewarning and to provide the opportunity to prevent the deleterious impact of impending leadership failure from negatively hitting your career, work life, or organization. At the minimum, knowing what failure resembles will permit you to prepare when you see it rolling your way. One can explore career options, prepare an exit strategy, or hunker down and shelter in place if forewarned of the cascade that flows from leadership failure. Think of using an umbrella in a downpour: You may be damp and uncomfortable, but you don't have to be drenched.

---

* Fenner, K., 2009.

Acknowledgments

Perhaps the most thanks belong to the many colleagues and clients whom we have known and with whom we have shared bread – among various libations in some cases – over the years, but whom, for reasons that should be obvious we cannot acknowledge. When we have acted and reacted in ways that we remain convinced were correct, ethical, and accurate, many (most?) are still identifiable as friends and colleagues. We are proud of their achievements and reactions to advice proffered when it was essential for their continuation in place and growth. Experiences we have shared with them often could be described as "owners' sleepless nights."

In addition, there have been a few standout critical readers and, in a few cases, anecdotal contributors whose efforts we'd like to acknowledge with thanks. You know how you have improved this work of ours even while we take full responsibility for the accuracy of reportage: While it seems a better road to follow to not tie you to particulars, we also accept the blame for errors of fact or judgment that remain.

Among those whose contributions to our stories or as reviewers remain undesignated are included with much appreciation: Peter Boumgarden, Nancy Barone, Robert S Brown, Thom Helm, T. Doug Lawson, and Gary L. Sharpe. While we accept full responsibility for what we have put between the covers of this work and regret any errors in fact or judgment, we also are clear that without the help of those named above and the unwitting help given by thousands with whom we have worked over our decades of service and consequent learning, this book could not have been written.

Finally, Kristine Medansky and her colleagues including Carly Cassano at Taylor & Francis, and especially Bryan Moloney at Deanta Global, have steered this work through the labyrinth of publishing to get the final product into your hands. Our thanks to them all.

Author Bios

> This week I achieved unprecedented levels of
> unverifiable productivity
>
> – Dilbert

Kate M. Fenner, RN, PhD

Having immersed herself in issues, innovations, and solutions
relevant to today's dynamic business, healthcare, and higher
educational organizations, Kate has the rare ability to problem-
solve with humor and deep analysis, communicating at all
levels of an organization – from frontline staff to the Board –
even when their goals seem unaligned. Aside from her former
CEO and Managing Director roles in the consulting world,
where she used her talents to help organizational clients meet
clinical, financial, and cultural goals, she has also held leadership roles for over a quarter century, including being a university Professor, Dean of Nursing, and Vice President, while
also serving on national and state boards and committees
focused on the advancement and support of education. She
has applied proven leadership and development strategies to a
wide range of hospitals, health systems, and academic medical
centers, providing clients with creative, effective solutions to
their most pressing organizational concerns, particularly focusing on leadership, organizational optimization, performance

improvement, and regulatory compliance. A model mentor for graduate students and a regular keynoter throughout the country, Kate authored a leading college text on law and ethics in healthcare, wrote numerous journal papers and blogs, and coauthored other professional works.

Mark W. Reifsteck, MHA, LFACHE

Mark has over 30 years of consistent leadership achievement in complex, value-based organizations and boutique consulting firms. His record includes excellent working relations with physicians, highlighting his skills in performance improvement methods to achieve strategic and operational results – especially where oppositional contentiousness had been entrenched. In not-for-profit hospital administration, he had increasing responsibilities starting at a 150-bed acute care general hospital, through assignments as SVP and COO at a top-10 integrated healthcare system, to Division President and Chief Executive at a 15-hospital system with $1.7 billion in net revenues, 14,000 employees, and 4000 physicians. He focused on improvements in market share, financial results, contracting, and clinical outcomes. In the for-profit sector, he worked through becoming Managing Director and President responsible for considerable corporate growth and systems improvements, while implementing improvements dedicated to activating the potential of healthcare organizations around the country. He is currently engaged in voluntary board work and other activities to advance his interests in philanthropy and healthcare innovation and constructive disruption. His publications reflect his awareness of industry changes and relevance of risk-taking.

Peter Fenner, PhD

Peter has decades of professional leadership experience within healthcare, higher education, corporate, and community environments. Heading various nationally funded research and organizational projects was a good background for later corporate leadership roles that also allowed him deep involvement in committees and boards of international, national, state, regional, and local associations. With early publications as a scientist, he mentored many doctoral learners and published dozens of journal articles and books as well a similar number of up to book-length proprietary reports. As Academic Vice-Chancellor within a Big-Ten System institution, a long-term Dean of Environmental and Applied Sciences, also with faculty roles in regional, state, and Ivy-league institutions, and having served as Executive Director of one of the U.S. College Commissions, and a corporate consulting leader, his abilities to work within a realm of competing and diverse interests allowed successful negotiation of difficult pathways. He has acted as lead consultant on a variety of projects involving communication systems, information systems/technology optimization, strategic planning, and management development initiatives. Current writing reflects his interest in leadership, linguistics, general semantics, and research methodologies.

Introduction

Our View: Why Us?

> I refuse to join any club that would have me...
>
> Telegram response to invitation to join Friar's Club
>
>   – Groucho Marx

As noted previously, the three of us have logged over 100 years of leadership experience in organizations from Health Systems to Universities to Corporations. We have served as company chief executives, health system leaders, and university officers. We've survived the myriad crises that befall companies, hospitals, and universities: Some inflicted by external events, many the result of poor, incompetent, or ill-informed leadership, occasionally even ours!

Since leaving institutional leadership we have applied the expertise (and the earned scar tissue) gained from these experiences to roles as strategic consultants to myriad complex organizations. Whether guiding CEOs, assisting with critical strategic change, or supporting leadership transitions,

DOI: 10.4324/9781003304371-1

1

we have had a privileged perch for observing the errors that cost organizations progress, reputation, and sometimes even existence.

Along this journey, we have witnessed and participated in spectacular leadership. We have also assisted organizations and surviving leaders in recovery from even more spectacular leadership failures. We have witnessed good, smart people foolishly execute dumb strategy and dull, unimpressive folks succeed spectacularly. Sometimes plain dumb luck is a key factor in leadership success or failure. Do not underestimate the role of chance in make-or-break leadership tenure. But to paraphrase Einstein, chance favors the prepared mind.

Can one increase the positive role of good luck in success? We think "yes," and will say more about that in the discussion of Leadership Attributes (*see Chapter 2*). But suffice it here to say that continuous attention to growth and development as a professional and as a person is a factor that favors better luck. One is never finished growing; whether working on a new skill, staying abreast of the latest knowledge, staying involved in community or professional organizations, all plow the ground for openness to new ideas and enhance the chances of good things happening.

From University Presidents who ignore the irresistible force of change to hospital Chief Executives who turn tone-deaf to input from key constituents to corporate managers unable to view the world through any but their own paradigms: There are many ways to fail but a few common threads to failure. Those common threads are teased out, identified, and defined to assist you, dear reader, in prevention and intervention in potential leadership fails.

The pleasure of being part of an effectively led organization and the techniques for emulating same have been well documented in myriad leadership texts. Such an experience provides a rich opportunity to learn and emulate the key characteristics of successful leaders. It can be a joy to be a team member in an organization with clarity of purpose, clear strategy, dedication to execution, and accountability for results.

There are common attributes of good leadership that can be learned and emulated. Storied leaders have transformed their experiences into multiple volumes of texts that yield observations of commonalities to achieve success.

We wanted to flip the paradigm and examine the characteristics of leadership failures, documenting the unique attributes of each, and suggest strategies for avoiding participating in, and much less, leading such disasters. Paraphrased: Success has many parents; failure is an orphan. We would add that the orphan has many cautionary tales to tell that inform and advise, sometimes more than success. Studying the orphans' stories lets us deduce commonalities of causation and routes to prevention.

We want to shine a light on the horrendous cost of failed leadership. This cost is not measured in dollars alone, although we do live in a society that monetizes almost every move, decision, or outcome. Failed leadership costs organizations resources, productivity, human capital/satisfaction, and even survival. We should also be appalled by the more important impact on people's lives, health, and at times actual existence.

Failure reverberates within an organizational system, impeding and destroying the ability to grow, function, and sometimes even exist. It also impacts members of the organization, the clients served, and the community where it exists. Leadership failure may seem to be an individual event, destroying career prospects or even ending a career. But the circle of influence is much larger – whether realized in economic or personal terms. Entire industries and communities have fallen victim to the errors of leaders. The pain of poor leadership is rarely simply felt by the so-called leader in question. In fact, that leader might effectively escape the results of poor decision-making, failed strategy, inept execution, or moral timidity, and go on to inflict those poor skills elsewhere while innocent – or at least less powerful – people experience the poor outcomes of that failed leadership. We have seen spectacularly incompetent leaders transition to new roles without accountability for past impact; much like head lice working their way across a kindergarten classroom, there are few ways to totally eliminate the impact of poor leadership.

Thus, this text – a compendium of leadership fails, an analysis of each and a framework for diagnosing and perhaps intervention in each. We will help the able reader avoid such fails. Minimally we give good guidance on when to bail out of a failing situation when control or influence over impending failure is minimal or nonexistent. We give guidance on how to diagnose impending inevitable failure and plan an exit strategy to avoid same. In the worst cases, perhaps we can assist with the identification of warning signs and permit preparation for failure and perhaps recovery in its aftermath.

Who are we to dole out leadership wisdom? After a succession of increasingly more complex healthcare management roles, Mark has served as Chief Operating Officer at a large, complex multi-hospital system, later as regional CEO for another system, and graduating from that experience he has applied his earned expertise to multiple consulting assignments. Peter is a veteran higher education leader, first as science faculty, then college Dean, and later as vice-chancellor in a state university system. Life after academe includes founding and selling a successful consultancy. Kate has been a hospital vice president, university faculty and Dean, and later university vice president before joining Peter (in life and business).

So why listen to us? Several reasons pop to mind. First and foremost, we are done with the journey, retired with no axe to grind, engagement to sell, or agenda to forward. We have had a fascinating set of careers, experienced brilliant leadership, and watched what leadership failure can do to an organization. Our only goal is to share this accumulated experience with the hope that the reader can avoid the same, change as needed, or at least temper a bad situation with a bit of foresight. Learn from our experiences, use the stretch marks we have earned to avoid that scar tissue, there will be plenty of other challenges to surmount.

Take the experience and use it or simply be entertained by the idiocy of others or design and implement a different idiocy. We have earned age and sagacity, use us to vicariously walk through the failures and learn from our time in the trenches. We do not have to temper our thoughts with consideration for the impact on our consulting portfolio, we are not promoting a paradigm for adoption that will lead potential clients to our door. In short, we are free of the financial and institutional constraints that bar many from revealing real attitudes and experiences. We are casting a look back over long and hopefully productive careers and sharing that view.

We anchor our leadership thoughts on a set of attributes that we believe are core to effective leadership. These attributes constitute our center of leadership necessities, the fundamental components that provide a baseline for success, and the absence of any provides the hole in the dike that allows the first trickle of water to begin to undermine the enterprise. In short, these attributes – honesty, self-awareness, emotional maturity, communication abilities, decisiveness, intelligence, and resilience – are core, are required, and constitute the North Star of successful leaders.

Book Organization and How to Use

This is a collection of short stories. Each one serves as an illustration of one or more serious leadership failures. Our goal is not to memorialize what might be considered "stupid leadership." Rather, we seek to depart from the leadership literature that wants to impress readers with *the* newest or historical *best* paradigm for leadership, with a litany of steps to be taken to follow as a formula to achieve leadership success. Our focus is on real-life situations that happen.

We'll assume that some combination of skills, experience, and good intentions have placed you into a leadership role.

Or you may be succeeding in a manager or practitioner role and evaluating the possibility of advancing to leadership in your discipline or organization: You may be seeking a larger portfolio. You may realize that a blunder is visible in your rear-view professional mirror (or have been caught at making same). Times and circumstances may have changed, regardless of why your shining star has lost its luster.

Although names, places, and professional settings may have been changed to protect identities and reputations, they all reflect real situations. The stories (vignettes) are of situations in process or beyond prevention. Remediation, damage control, and resetting of reputation may now be your focus.

Our vignettes, then, set the stage, define one or more significant failures, and in boxed comments offer some thoughts about prevention, damage control, or "nexts."

Each of the vignettes starts off with a pithy epigraph perhaps to remind readers of why they are reading ahead! The graphic that follows is intended as a "do-it-yourself exercise" to help you focus on how various leadership (failure) traits may or may not be impacting you as a leader, or your organization through your leadership. Each ends with an attempt to reflect usefully on the story's history, outcomes, and relationship to *your* future.

Vignettes and other content need not be read in the sequence presented. Sections may easily be skipped or read out of turn. Each section should stand on its own merits.

Following the vignettes section, you will find essays that peer more closely at each of the seven attributes that we consider essential to avoid failure. These should be in your headlights as you move beyond your "troubles" of the past or plan on strategies for avoiding future challenges.

The graphic serves as a reminder of how others' failures can be tied to their embrace or disdain of traits highlighted. The challenge is essentially a thought-provocation to determine how you, personally, and your organization, specifically, would relate to the attributes as exemplified in behaviors, processes, and outcomes that might parallel the stories told in our vignettes. Fill them in with check marks or comments as you contemplate; they may be helpful in plotting your own "next" actions.

The concluding text (*Chapter 5*) serves to summarize lessons learnable, as well a very important component of leadership – important for the individual and the institution, and any desired legacy of successes: Succession.

STORIES 1

The stories that follow are real, perhaps amusing in hind-sight, and instructive for application to other settings. We have encountered, helped correct, and survived all of the situations that follow.

The limitations and leadership defects that these stories illustrate are not unique, were predictable, and probably pre-ventable given a hint of self-awareness (we'll discuss leader-ship attributes such as self-awareness later).

Please read these stories both for amusement and instruc-tion. If you recognize yourself, excellent! This will give you an opportunity to reflect, consider corrective actions, and apply lessons to your own career. If you recognize behaviors exhibited within your team, you'll have the opportunity to coach others, prevent poor outcomes, and support growth. If you recognize behaviors of a superior leader, then you need to decide if this is a "kiss of death" potential problem; or, is it something that you can manage to work around?

If you note the applicability of these lessons to your orga-nization and the behavior is outside your control (i.e., another division, or reflected in a superior), you have serious choices to make. Is this behavior in contrast to organizational pol-icy? Is this behavior potentially destructive of organizational aims? Is this behavior correctable with coaching or other

DOI: 10.4324/9781003304371-2

intervention? Am I in a position to impact change positively? Will intervention have blowback consequences on me and my position?

All of these are complex questions, and answers require careful thought and perhaps guidance from a very trusted coach or mentor. Understand that pointing out the deficits of others can have devastating consequences, particularly for the person doing the pointing! Go carefully here, but do not ignore your sense of responsibility. It is best to approach the recognition of organizational or personal risk by first assuring that your assessment is valid and then assuming the mantle of a diplomat: How best to seek change without negative blowback.

Chapter 1

Vignettes About Failures

What's a vignette, you might ask? Well…it's another word for story…but a particular kind of short story…one designed to offer meaning using provocative imagery. In this case, the imagery is based on failure, specifically leadership failures. Why would we use stories of failures in a book about leadership?

Failure is a popular topic in the business literature. Much is written about technology companies, in particular making a virtue of failure. Some companies create incentives to encourage their employees to try, fail, iterate, and try again – constantly improving a product until they get something that the market will value. This is a phenomenon we've seen referred to as "failing fast, failing forward."

The type of failure we are referring to is different from essentially a series of controlled experiments where you test your hypothesis – see how it works and adjust till you get the result you are looking for.

The kind of management failure we describe relates to a failure of character or, as the lawyers might describe it, willful negligence. This type of failure issues from a lack of poorly formed leadership traits of honesty, self-awareness, and emotional maturity, among the others, we describe in the text.

This type of failure consciously ignores advice or contrarian data and leads to the pursuit of a path that ultimately ends in harm to the organization, harm to other employees, and harm to the executive pursuing that path in a word:Failure.

In the world of politics, we don't think it should be controversial to describe the Watergate debacle and the role of Richard Nixon as a monumental leadership failure. The events of Watergate resulted in multiple resignations, jail sentences, and the resignation in disgrace of President Nixon himself. In addition to the hearings held at the time, there have been exhaustive historical accounts of what happened--describing who did what and an attempt to frame why it occurred. An inescapable conclusion is that a deeply flawed leader used his considerable influence and authority to compel action that ended in one of the biggest political scandals in the history of our country.

In the business world, a similarly infamous series of leadership failures resulted in the collapse of Enron and the destruction of untold millions of dollars of value for leaders, employees, and investors alike. Detailed forensic accounts of what happened and who did what have been well documented. Careers were ruined, senior executives went to jail, and countless numbers of investors lost their stake in the company. We don't think it is too simplistic to conclude that it was a fundamental failure of leaders within Enron that led to the events that resulted in the destruction of the company and assuring the name Enron will forever be synonymous with corrupt leadership and catastrophic failure.

The failures recounted here do not reflect the notoriety of Watergate or Enron but were and are just as impactful for the organizations involved. There are leadership lessons to be drawn from headlines and applied to organizations. But there are also myriad everyday examples of leaders behaving badly, without deep thought or moral compass that provide useful instruction.

It's not that we won't fail. All professionals have some stumbles on their career path. Anyone saying otherwise is dis-assembling. But the key is what we learn from our failures and from the failures of others, and how we incorporate lessons and learnings from stumbles into our path moving forward. The achievement is what we learn from those failures and how we turn those lessons into success that is important.

Please recognize that the presentation of possible stories that follow could seem endless. We've limited these to shorter essays that are intended to be pointed, impactful, and lead to positive introspection and – when necessary – change.

The stories we tell in the following section are intended to help the reader learn from others' mistakes in the hope that they won't make the same ones themselves. That's a tall order since we seemed programmed to think "that can't happen to me."

In short, we hope our stories convince you "oh yes it can!" Regardless, we trust you will find these stories of interest and learning as you progress on your leadership journey.

Vignette 1: Well-prepared for the Wrong Role

Right Church; Wrong Pew

– Anonymous

Failed Essential Attribute	Honesty	Self-awareness	Emotional Maturity	Communicator	Decisiveness	Intelligence	Resilience
This vignette							

Management and leadership require discipline, knowledge, and an applicable skill set that can be studied and practiced. Thus, effective leadership requires learning and multiple skills. But most of all it requires the ability to "put yourself out there," to risk being wrong, looking a bit foolish, and at times admitting that while you don't have all the answers, you will seek out help to find them. Two stories of overly well-defended egos have in the background leaders who may be prone to indicating that they've never made mistakes, cannot say, "I don't know," and are certain that all failures should be attributed anywhere else but to them.

One rarely, if ever, encounters a born leader. Common myths often present the image of a "born leader," the great man born to the role of inspiring others to engage in the pursuit of a higher goal. In reality, leaders don't arise without first mastering the set of attributes inherent to the role.

Occasionally, an organization's Board or senior leaders will assume that if someone is a master of the work of the organization they can lead in the organization. Too often, this proves disastrous. Promoting a skilled professional to the supervision of other professionals requires more than mastery of the mission of the organization. Leadership requires study and experience beyond certification in the work of the company.

This failure happens when a beloved and erudite faculty member is promoted to academic leadership without preparation or mentoring for the role. Hospitals and health systems frequently assume that a well-respected physician who has accomplished much in clinical practice will make a good leader for an administrative role. Profession-based firms, such as law firms, accounting firms, consultancies, frequently select a practitioner from their ranks who has been a "rainmaker" (prolific in key client acquisition) or has had a star turn in a high-profile case or special assignment as the firm's key leader. All these examples demonstrate leader selection based on an incomplete picture of the road to becoming a real leader. Neglecting to support leadership development prior to placement in a senior role is a frequent cause of failure.

> *Example*: A respected senior physician has been a stalwart member of the medical staff for decades. He has earned the regard of peer physicians and hospital leaders alike. The role of CEO opens, and a well-meaning but uninformed Board decides to place the dear doctor in the position.
>
> Confronted with responsibilities and content that is unfamiliar and forced to confront decisions that are outside of his experience, he reverts to the behaviors that assured success in his previous clinical life: Giving orders and expecting rapid results. Subordinates with expertise in areas where he is ill-prepared are not consulted, but instead are simply commanded to actions he believes will result in accomplishing the task at hand.
>
> Unfortunately, leading a complex system composed of variant-required inputs is not conducive to top-down order-based leadership. Failing to seek the

input of others results in a series of disastrous financial and strategic decisions.

Another Example: A quite bright and well-educated consultant was great at diagnosing others' organizational problems. He was a genius at institutional post-mortem, figuring out what others had done or failed to do that initiated a crisis, impeded success, or initiated a shortfall. His peers were very impressed with this talent, certain he might be just the one to lead their organization to success.

If he could analyze others' failures so adeptly, he certainly would be able to lead their growing company to success.

Things began with promise: Effective sales teams would land solid assignments, and he was good at deploying and leading consulting teams through the inevitable challenges of helping others. So, the collected partners decided that engagements would be even more effective if he joined in sales efforts.

Suddenly he hit the wall. Totally unable to deploy the brilliant insights he made to colleagues, he stumbled and stammered on sales calls, frequently becoming withdrawn and silent in the presence of a prospective client's senior leaders. His efforts to provide direction to deployed teams soon began to fade. It seemed that as he became more visible as a leader, he also became less capable. What happened to the insightful, erudite professional?

He had hit his deepest vulnerability: The intense fear of public failure. Though able to adroitly measure others' issues and challenges, he was paralyzed by the fear of his own error or failure. Reflection on his preparation for this leadership role revealed that he had spent his career successfully critiquing the performance of others, but never able to take risks of his own. He was hobbled by fear of inadequacy, of looking less than perfect.

By the time the Board becomes aware of the CEO's unsuccessful tenure, much organizational damage has occurred. Good senior leaders have left, others have been driven to dysfunction while hiding from the wrath of the CEO. The result is an unsuccessful CEO, a ruined professional career, and an organization with a severely impaired future.

Leadership requires acknowledging that while you don't have all the answers, you are willing to learn; it is also knowing when to take appropriate risks, how to manage failure, and being able to publicly admit to shortcomings or errors and resolving to address the same.

Vignette 2: Counter-cultural Leadership

> The culture of any organization is shaped by the worst
> behavior the leader is willing to tolerate
> – Gruenther and Whittaker, Indiana State University

Failed Essential Attribute	Honesty	Self-awareness	Emotional Maturity	Communicator	Decisiveness	Intelligence	Resilience
This vignette							

Culture has been described "as the way we do things around
here." That is, there are certain ways people act, make decisions, and comport themselves in the organization.

Some organizations are very buttoned up and formal; and,
many organizations today are consciously trying to be more laid
back and informal. This can be reflected in how people dress
and how they communicate with each other and senior leaders.

Organizational culture can be a function of the influence of
the CEO, or the Board and in faith-based organizations by the
founders of the organization. A new leader in an organization
will make a big effort to understand the culture and any behavioral norms that go with it. Something as simple as starting and
ending meetings on time may be part of the culture; so might
rules about using cellphones onsite and at meetings – be they
in-person or virtual. How complex decisions are made might
have normative behaviors that it would be good to understand
before undertaking a task such as an acquisition. Being tone-
deaf or willfully ignoring the cultural norms of an organization
is usually an unforgiveable error when made by a new leader.

Example: A faith-based organization with which we
are familiar intentionally hired leaders who were

diverse in their faith backgrounds but shared a similar value system. For reasons that were unique to one leader, she ignored the faith-based norms of the organization and made decisions in conflict with the organization's cultural norms and even their values. In one circumstance, she advocated to just cancel a contract with a valued partner – without cause – and said that the vendor could just sue the organization if they didn't like it.

After repeated efforts to communicate this divergence from cultural norms and values and efforts to coach the leader into normative behavior, the leader exited the organization. Although nothing illegal or immoral was perpetrated by this leader, her actions didn't match the cultural norms of the organization, and the dissonance her actions had created had become intolerable over time.

Another example: In another organization, the leader repeatedly tried to hire his spouse into a senior leader role despite organization prohibitions against this practice. The leader ultimately was not able to hire his spouse, but it created tremendous tension for other senior leaders, and ultimately undermined their confidence in the judgment of the leader, impacting his ability to lead effectively. This among other decisions and behavior eventually led to this leader's departure from the organization.

Ignoring cultural norms can have real and negative impacts on a new leader's effectiveness and success in an organization. Additionally, it can hurt morale throughout the organization.... It is important to understand these cultural norms and learn to work within them.

Vignette 3: Well Qualified, But Lazy

Lazy is a very strong word, I like to call it *'selective participation'*

– Garfield

Failed Essential Attribute	Honesty	Self-awareness	Emotional Maturity	Communicator	Decisiveness	Intelligence	Resilience
This vignette							

Being smart and well trained are important attributes in successful leaders. However, if intelligence and good training aren't coupled with an appropriate work ethic, the likelihood of success in an organization is diminished.

A very smart, well-trained, and educated leader with whom we are familiar is an articulate and charismatic individual who was quite charming in his conversations. He was up on the current industry trends and topics, and could speak with authority about his particular field. However, he seemed to enjoy the trappings of his office entirely too much; and, frequently he only "dialed in" his performance on many days, pouting and acting aggrieved when compelled to actually do his own work.

By all objective measures, this person had appropriate training and experience for the position; however, sufficient diligence wasn't performed on the leader's previous work experience and history.

What the organization found out later was that this leader used all manner of manipulation and evasion to avoid doing his own work. He was also known to take frequent "business"-related trips and seminars. It was rumored that he didn't attend the seminars, but instead spent his time at the pool or other personal diversions...all on the company credit card.

This leader was self-aware enough to know that he needed an enabler to do his work for him and to make excuses during his frequent unexplained absences. This leader routinely had his second in command attend meetings on his behalf, finish his reports or do them altogether, and then cover for him at meetings that he was expected to attend. The leader, however, was articulate, charming, had an excellent sense of timing about when to appear for high-profile events, and was able to "baffle with BS," as the saying goes.

Because the second in command enabled this behavior and covered over the leader's lapses, this behavior was allowed to continue for several years. Over time, however, the circle of people who were aware of this behavior grew larger to the point the leader couldn't hide his management negligence and he exited the organization.

The damage to the organization that this behavior created was incalculable. Morale of his subordinates was deeply impaired and progress on key initiatives was slowed or halted because he wasn't driving the changes he was supposed to create. Once the organization decided to take action about this leader, unhealthy turnover occurred and those who remained had their confidence shaken in the organization and its mission and values.

Intellectual acuity and good training are not sufficient to being an effective leader. A strong work ethic must also accompany those traits. When a lazy leader is enabled by others in the organization, the inequity of the situation will ultimately cause great harm in that organization.

Vignette 4: Sick Organization Syndrome (SOS)

> Some of the most poisonous people come disguised as bosses
>
> – Anonymous

Failed Essential Attribute	Honesty	Self-awareness	Emotional Maturity	Communicator	Decisiveness	Intelligence	Resilience
This vignette							

All too many CEOs have bought into the popular "cult of personality," and the celebrity CEO ethic is pervasive in the business and popular literature. It is very hard for leaders to remain immune to the siren song of praise and adulation from sycophants and others trying to curry favor. This has become especially true in the age of social media with the psychic rewards of instantaneous recognition. The issue is especially pernicious when the leader sees all issues through the lens of "...how does it make me look."

Often overlooked is that unchecked, executive hubris can generate a host of troubles in an organization we call Sick Organization Syndrome (SOS). As the well-known acronym implies – when this happens it is time to call for emergency help or abandon ship for the lifeboats!

To be sure, being in leadership roles requires a strong sense of self – it would be crippling to be plagued with self-doubt and low levels of confidence in a top leadership role. Also, a large part of executive work is organizing and influencing others to perform the key functions of the organization. When this is done well and appropriately, it can be thought of as benevolent manipulation, that is, causing people to achieve the organization's goals through appropriate and healthy leadership.

It can be particularly difficult for Boards and other leaders to recognize when a strong sense of self turns narcis-
sistic and when influencing others turns to more malignant
manipulation.

> A large outwardly successful organization with
> which are familiar was led by a CEO who so thor-
> oughly aligned his ego with the organization that
> anything he did that was good for him was – by
> definition – good for the organization. This took
> many forms including continually seeking out and
> gaining external praise and recognition for his
> achievements. Seeking out that praise was a worthy
> pursuit when he was outwardly praised or recog-
> nized, for in his view it necessarily brought that same
> praise and recognition to the organization.
> A flaw in this thinking was that the logic did not
> extend to other senior leaders. When other lead-
> ers also gained external or, for that matter, internal
> recognition for their accomplishments – if it was
> perceived by the CEO that a subordinate's light was
> shining as bright or brighter than his own, he would
> find ways to criticize or discredit that leader – the
> more publicly the better. It was a familiar pattern that
> the CEO made himself feel more secure by creating
> insecurity among his subordinates. Over time, this
> resulted in diminished executive morale and predict-
> ably higher-than-normal turnover in the senior leader
> ranks. This negative effect trickled down to other
> layers of the organization as well.
> The best time to identify if an organization has SOS
> is before you join it. Unfortunately, there is no defini-
> tive test for this condition; however, there are signs and
> symptoms to which a person should pay attention.
> When doing your research on an organization you
> might want to join, test the environment to see how

high a public profile the CEO maintains. Does the
CEO seem to crave that notoriety, or is it a natural
function of his/her role in the community as a result
of leading that kind of organization? Is the CEO the
only person with a large public profile or are there
others? If you interview in the organization, can you
sense genuine warmth among the senior leaders or is
it more "pro forma"? What has been the senior leader
turnover over the past 5–10 years? Does it seem
unusually high? Are these voluntary or involuntary
departures? Answers to these questions may help you
build a profile of what type of organization this is
and if you want to be a part of it.

Another example of an indispensable CEO
follows: The ego-driven CEO's impact can extend
well beyond the boundaries of his organization
and impact the community or industry at large.
Recognizing this deleterious influence can be difficult, minimizing the impact even more complex.

We were asked to facilitate the alliance of five
similar companies into a regional consortium able to
compete in the industry sector on a national level.
The organizations had significant benefits to be realized from the relationship. All were solid players in
their markets with little geographic overlap in areas
served. Each had distinct expertise in varying service
lines of the industry. All had the financial where-
withal to invest resources to support the alliance.
There was a significant upside to the potential relationship and little downside risk. Yet the consortium
fell apart, crashing on the ego of one of the CEOs
involved. Though his was the smallest organization
by financial and service volume measures, he was
the undisputed "King" of his realm, all institutional
decisions reflected his imprint and served to highlight his genius.

As the larger consortium began to emerge from discussions the subject of who would serve as chair became a topic. Interestingly the two CEOs of the two largest players demurred the honor, even though either would have been the logical choice of any outside viewer. The third and fourth organizational CEOs were neutral on who should chair. But the CEO of the smallest organization became irate, insisting that only he could serve as chair or the organization could not move forward. His display of ego was sufficiently off-putting as to cause a pause in the formation while the other four leaders reflected on their ability to commit to the emergent consortium. Eventually, talks cooled as participants realized that this issue of who leads and the recalcitrant fairly childish behavior was a harbinger of future issues. You can guess the result. One strong egocentric leader terminated the forward motion and cost the community the benefits that this consortium might have delivered.

A strong ego is a prerequisite to effective organizational leadership, but perversely, too strong an ego will warp and eventually harm the organization being led.

If you are unfortunate enough to find yourself in an organization with this kind of leadership, there are no good choices. You can either do your best to insulate yourself from this malignant leader or you must accept the situation and begin to plan your exit as soon as possible. In rare circumstances, others in the organization can try to go around the leader to the governing Board, but that is a very fraught tactic. Boards have often already been co-opted by this leader and are unaware of these tactics. In addition, if the CEO finds out that you went around him to the Board, it will most likely not go well for you and your continued tenure at the organization.

Vignette 5: Large and In Charge

> Often, poor leadership is masked by those with the loudest voices.
>
> – Nick Fewings

Failed Essential Attribute	Honesty	Self-awareness	Emotional Maturity	Communicator	Decisiveness	Intelligence	Resilience
This vignette							

There are times in an organization's life when it may be challenged by an existential threat. It could be a new competitor taking market share, it might be a run on cash, or a regulatory infraction threatening to shut down an operating unit. Whatever the crisis, leadership is tasked with quickly assessing the threat then developing and executing countermeasures to offset that threat. The types of leaders needed in a turnaround situation are different than the leadership style needed in times of relative stability and prosperity.

Someone who can take strong command of the situation and give firm direction to staff to assure that the threat is beaten back is required. However, when the threat has receded, that leadership style isn't as effective in more normal operating times, thus the ability to moderate your style is essential to longer-term success.

The "command and control" leadership style may well be needed during a crisis. However, when the crisis has passed, a return to a more participative style may be appropriate. Not every leader is able to make that pivot, but one such individual did. The example below is of a potentially large failure being turned onto a significant success.

In one circumstance, a physician leader we know had unquestionable clinical competence in his field of practice. He was an engaging individual who maintained strict control over the operating environment he worked in. He did not suffer fools well and could be biting and hurtful in his criticism of subordinates' performance.

His argument defending this behavior was that he was dealing with life and death with his patients, and he was "captain of the ship" and wasn't running a democracy! Because he achieved great clinical results, this behavior, although disruptive and destructive of the team, was tolerated in the organization. Over time, however, members of the team lost patience with being verbally abused, and in one case physically threatened, and finally reported his abusive behavior.

It was at this time that the physician was required to alter his style or risk having his position eliminated. He chose wisely in this case and altered his leadership style.

Even in high-risk environments such as an operating room, we now know that the old "captain of the ship" model of leadership doesn't always work. Input from others participating in the surgery is often essential for a positive outcome. In fact, studies of grievous surgical errors such as wrong-site surgery have demonstrated that open communication and encouragement of a "see something, say something" attitude will diminish surgical errors.

And of course, abusive behavior of any kind should always be addressed directly.

It is worth reiterating here that all leadership failures don't have to be terminal to your career. In the case above, the physician was generally behaving in the way he had been acculturated to behave by his colleagues. Authoritarian, and at times abusive, behavior has for too long been tolerated in health-care organizations. Slowly and unevenly across organizations that is changing. Fortunately, the physician in this case was fundamentally a good and caring individual and when confronted with the harmful impacts of his behavior on others, he accepted coaching to alter that behavior. His transformation wasn't a straight line and he had to self-correct from time to time, but he did make the turn. Not all failure is final, but without subsequent changes, it can be.

Also, there have been very publicly reported instances when an airline captain who would not be overridden or approached about an impending failure or danger point allowed a flight to become a crisis and then a crash.

The largest loss-of-life airline accident, in Tenerife, 1977, with 583 fatalities, was caused when the captain of one plane, the KLM 747, demanded takeoff implementation of his crew despite lack of clearance from the control tower. The "I'm in charge!" decision coupled with fog combined to create a horrific, avoidable loss of life.

Compare this to other publicly reported incidents when pilots in charge have remained calm, taken in, and requested help and inputs for precise and accurate decisions to be made in a timely manner that resulted in no losses of life or limb. (Think: Captain Chesley Sullenberger landing his disabled domestic airliner on the Hudson River in New York, with all the salutatory aftermath.)

In times of crisis, a more authoritarian style may be appropriate, but in a normal operating environment a more participative approach will likely be more successful.

Vignette 6: Weak Moral Compass

> A sense of shame is not a bad moral compass
> – Colin Powell

Failed Essential Attribute	Honesty	Self-awareness	Emotional Maturity	Communicator	Decisiveness	Intelligence	Resilience
This vignette							

The lure of seemingly easy material gain among people can be irresistible. Without even stronger organizational controls, executives can oftentimes be enticed to step over the line and enrich themselves inappropriately.

Unfortunately, there are no shortages of examples of this type of behavior in organizations. Daily there are reports of disgraced executives fired and even prosecuted for illegally enriching themselves at the expense of the organization. We are aware of executives who did business with their paramours and took kickbacks from their companies. We know of bosses who set up shell vendors and bought bogus supplies from those vendors and pocketed the change. We came across an executive who inflated her expense reports to cover personal family trips and sporting activities. The list is literally endless of the larceny that occurs in organizations and is often perpetrated by the very executives entrusted to run the enterprise.

The key question for the aspiring executive is "how do I avoid being similarly tempted" when an opportunity presents itself – and we promise – if you work in large organizations long enough you will have opportunities!

Having a strong organizational moral compass means understanding the fiduciary responsibility you have to protect organizational assets and acting accordingly.

It is our belief that most people don't start work with the mindset that they intend to defraud their organization. There may be sociopaths like that, but in our experience, the vast majority of people believe themselves to be honest, hardworking folks who get up every day wanting to do good work... and most of the time do just that.

> *Example.* However, there are several common traps that can lure a person into a pattern of dishonest behavior. Expense accounts come to mind. If there is a culture of "padding expense accounts" in your organization, it can be very easy to rationalize doing this yourself because "everybody does it," and it really doesn't hurt anyone. This is the slope the executive above slipped on when she gradually inflated her expense accounts to steal millions of dollars from her organization and ultimately went to jail. Expense accounts are the easiest place to start...fill them out in a timely fashion, and accurately follow the company's policy...period!
>
> *Another example.* Another trap an aspiring executive can fall into is being asked by a senior executive to do something inappropriate, then thinking that you will do it just to go along to get along. This could be something as simple as backdating a contract or countersigning an expense that you know is inflated or inappropriate. Even if you are not profiting from the inappropriate action, you enable it by going along with the expectation that your career will be enhanced by the executives asking you to do

this action. This can be harder to resist if you fear that your career may hang in the balance.

An organization we know had a CEO who pressured his CFO into backdating lease dates on contracts in order to clean up a regulatory deficiency that could have cost the organization many thousands of dollars in fines. The CFO fearing for his job complied with the request. The whole scheme ultimately fell apart, both executives were fired, and the organization still had to pay fines. All of this could have been avoided by owning up to the error (it was an error of omission). In fact, there was a safe harbor for such errors, and it could have been remediated without anyone losing their jobs!

Many companies have a compliance officer or legal counsel that you could turn to in order to report this activity or seek guidance on how to proceed. These are very hard things to deal with in an organization, and it is nearly impossible to process the right thing to do by yourself. It is best to seek counsel within your organization or use a trusted external advisor if you have one.

Regardless, if you slip down that slope with the person perpetrating the illegal scheme, it is very easy to become implicated in it and risk your own career and reputation.

One more example. Many organizations have rules and regulations focused on expense reimbursement. Most follow an "honor system" for enforcement, asking individuals to submit expense statements to a superior for sign-off with little scrutiny. The vast majority of folks follow the rules and honestly submit expense recounting. However, a slight inflation of expenses can be a temptation for even a usual straight-arrow employee.

We were providing consultative support to a large, leading, organization when an illustrative incident occurred. A senior vice president submitted an outlandish reimbursement of expense request. The request triggered an inquiry from the financial side of the house. A retrospective review yielded information documenting a trail of gradually inflating expense requests that culminated in the outlandish one that triggered the review. The senior vice president had been "padding" his expenses for years. The estimated total inflation was in the many thousands of dollars.

He was immediately dismissed by the CEO, and an interim executive was placed to assess other operational issues and potential areas of conflict.

That assessment led to the revelation that the ex-SVP was accepting gifts of travel from vendors, had steered a minor supply contract to a distant relative, and cast doubt on several development deals he had initiated. The reveal of his cheating damaged internal morale and slowed future business initiatives while additional vetting of decisions was completed and caused implementation of a much more draconian approval system for expenses and contracting.

What had begun as a little inflation of expenses ended a career and hugely impacted an entire organization. This incident well documents the slippery slope effect, or as grandmother said, "You can't be a little bit pregnant!" Once you cheat a little, the path is known.

In business as in most walks of life…honesty is still the best policy…you need your own personal and organizational guardrails to keep your career on track.

Vignette 7: You Can Stay Too Long

> Too many pieces of music finish too long after the end
> – Igor Stravinsky

Failed Essential Attribute	Honesty	Self-awareness	Emotional Maturity	Communicator	Decisiveness	Intelligence	Resilience
This vignette							

Lulled by the trappings of office and lack of better alternatives, many executives give in to the temptation to stay in their positions well past their contribution of value.

In jobs that require physical effort (strength, mobility, endurance), there is a certain obsolescence that tells you (or those around you) when it is time to stop doing that work or look for another position. Athletics provide lots of examples here. In jobs that are more cognitive in nature, that obsolescence may not be as obvious. Again, examples abound of physicians losing a step but still able to function, teachers not as sharp but can still do their work. Senior executives are no different.

> *Example.* The CEO of a health organization we know removed a long-tenured senior executive in her organization. When relaying the story to a colleague, the response was, "you can stay too long, can't you?" We think the answer to this is a resounding yes.
>
> Although anecdotal, it seems to us that in many work environments, 70 has become the new 65 when it comes to senior executive retirement age. And why not? With hand-picked board members that don't challenge you, and with all the perks of office – including hefty salaries – why would you step away? Our perspective here isn't ageist – after all, the three of us are north (or well north) of 65. Rather, our view

is that the intellectual and physical rigors of running large, complex organizations require energy, flexibility of intellect, and stamina that biology teaches us decline the older you get. There is a body of evidence that supports our view.*

Hanging on to your position only because you can, doesn't seem to us fair to the organization and its future leaders.

This can be a very uncomfortable situation to confront in an organization or in yourself, but it is nevertheless important. Although there is no one test to determine whether someone has stayed too long in her role, there are some telltale signs.

Does the executive keep current with industry developments, or has he already learned all he thinks he needs to, and he just plays the same old tapes of the way things used to be?

Does the executive keep tight control on most decision-making and isn't seen as a mentor to younger executives?

Have the executive's work habits been altered: Perhaps coming in later, leaving earlier, delegating key ceremonial roles to others?

If any of this resonates in your organization or with yourself, it is time to take stock and realistically begin planning an exit strategy. If you fail to do so, our experience teaches us that at some point you will get the tap on the shoulder and be told it is your time to exit the stage, ready or not.

> Failure to have a plan of succession for your organization or yourself puts the organization and your career at risk of unplanned obsolescence.

---

* Brooks, Arthur C., 2019

Vignette 8: Symbols and Behaviors Communicate More Than Words

> Symbols are powerful because they are visible signs of invisible realities
>
> – St. Augustine

Failed Essential Attribute	Honesty	Self-awareness	Emotional Maturity	Communicator	Decisiveness	Intelligence	Resilience
This vignette							

Leaders are constantly communicating their values, views, and priorities, whether intentionally or inadvertently.

Whether through symbols, behaviors, or decisions, the leaders and organization's values are communicated in myriad ways – the least of which may be through words. Spoken values need to match behaved values, else only the behavior will communicate. A leader who says he values diversity of thought and then surrounds himself with "yes men" who parrot his conclusions and praise his brilliance, clearly communicates little regard for the spoken value of diversity of thought. His followers soon understand not to disagree or offer alternative thoughts.

Entire organizations can betray their stated values through operational decisions. If an organization lays claim to a value of "putting employees first," yet demonstrates little regard for employee welfare through seemingly draconian bottom-line-focused human resource management decisions, then the actual value is revealed regardless of stated values.

The greater the visibility of the leader, the more scrutiny will be paid to her or his behavior by members of the

organization. Top of the house positions bear the most examination. Occupants of "Chief of ..." roles are watched for cues
and behavior giving meaning to team members who follow.
So even the slightest deviation from an intended direction can
upend a leader's directional intent.

>*Example*: The University is having a very challeng-
>ing fiscal year due to external forces (changes in
>state and federal tuition support) and internal fac-
>tors such as recruiting students from more economi-
>cally challenged backgrounds. The senior leadership
>announces an across-the-board compensation
>freeze, halting new staff recruitment and vigorously
>diminishing any and all expenses. The week after
>announcing the austerity measures, the President
>parks his new luxury sedan, an annual gift of a well-
>intended Trustee, in his usual reserved spot. Faculty
>and staff become outraged at what is perceived as
>a flaunting of privilege by the President, meetings
>ensue, memos fly, the student newspaper covers
>the controversy prominently and finally the Board
>receives a signed letter of no confidence from the
>faculty concerning the President's leadership during
>difficult times.
>
>*Additional example*: After a difficult quarter in
>terms of financial operations, a nationally renowned
>non-profit organization draws various constituents –
>members, employees, volunteers – to its corporate
>headquarters to brainstorm cost reduction and rev-
>enue enhancement alternatives. At the close of an
>exhausting and somewhat discouraging conference,
>the organization's CEO takes the dais to announce
>a new set of belt-tightening rules for all. Among
>the various regulations were rather draconian

clampdowns on travel expenses, despite that travel to member organizations is a key necessity of viability. After learning of the new restrictive policies on transport and daily living expenses, a group of employees and volunteers pool to await a shuttle bus to the airport. While waiting, they observe a stretch-limo pull to the front entrance as the CEO enters the car for his trip home.

> What an impactful message about cost management!

Vignette 9: A Single Source of Truth Needs to be Verified

> The reason I talk to myself is because I'm the only one whose answers I accept
>
> – George Carlin

Failed Essential Attribute	Honesty	Self-awareness	Emotional Maturity	Communicator	Decisiveness	Intelligence	Resilience
This vignette							

Senior leaders cannot be experts in all operations under their purview.

It behooves a leader to rely on the expertise and judgment of subordinates with specialty preparation in appropriate fields. However, it is imperative to have validated not only the competence of selected subordinates but also the veracity of information provided by same. Ronald Reagan's oft-quoted exhortation to "Trust but verify" is aptly applied here.

> *Example*: A well-seasoned hospital system CEO is superb at strategy, inspiring followers and negotiating with corporate system authorities for support and resources. She is not comfortable with the minutiae of financial management in a complex health system, but has come to rely heavily on the judgment and authority of her regional Chief Financial Officer. Though reliable in most arenas, he is not an experienced contract negotiator and agrees to a disadvantageous contract with a major payor. His representation to the CEO is that the arrangement will be revenue neutral to the organization. Accepting his assurance without external

validation leads her to sign the contract. The system
loses multiple millions over the course of two years,
the corporate parent becomes concerned and terminates the trusting regional CEO over the incident.

In the field of forensic accounting, there is something called
the "Fraud Triangle." It is a model to describe what the con-
ditions are for fraud to happen in organizations and how to
prevent and detect it.

The first condition is the opportunity. Organizations that
have weak internal controls, segregation of duties or of good
oversight provide fertile ground for fraud to occur. This lays the
groundwork for a motivated employee or vendor to take advantage of weak internal control processes to perpetrate a fraud.

Motivation, the second condition, can come from many
sources, such as disgruntled employees who are not being
paid what they believe they are worth...or maybe they have
had a personal setback financially and see the company as
a quick way to meet that shortfall...often with the inten-
tion of paying it back...which leads to the third condition
– rationalization.

Over time, the person may rationalize that the amount
stolen was small and insignificant...or that only a little more
time is needed to pay it back...or maybe their anger with the
company allows them to convince themselves they are owed
the amount. This cycle has played out in organizations seemingly forever.

A not-for-profit with which we are familiar
employed a well-respected woman in a bookkeep-
ing role – she worked for the company for many
years and was liked by all. The company was small
and couldn't afford a lot of staff. Consequently,
this beloved and respected person handled almost

all the duties related to receiving cash donations, including recording and depositing those donations in the bank. Unbeknownst to others, the woman enjoyed the occasional trip to the casino and over time built up credit card debt to finance her gambling habit. The weight of that debt caused her to look to her employer as a place to find cash to finance her losses. Eventually, she rationalized this theft by reasoning that she had been underpaid all along and was really owed this money. Finally, the cash disparities became too big to ignore by senior leaders and the scheme fell apart with the woman ultimately going to jail for her actions. That was harmful enough, but the organization and its mission were deeply impaired financially and also reputationally among their donors and those receiving services.

Good leaders recognize that everyone is human, including themselves, hence prone to failure. For that reason, they endorse and demand that accountability systems be put in place to help keep honest people honest. We all need guardrails to help keep us on course – financial accountability systems are a way to accomplish that.

> Using outside expertise, trusted advisors, or consultants allows a leader to be assured that information and guidance provided by even close lieutenants is valid.

Vignette 10: Temper Tantrums Are for Two-Year-Olds

> Wars and temper tantrums are the makeshifts of igno-
> rance; regrets are illuminations come too late
> — Joseph Campbell

Failed Essential Attribute	Honesty	Self-awareness	Emotional Maturity	Communicator	Decisiveness	Intelligence	Resilience
This vignette							

Senior executive positions are often stress-intensive with multiple agenda items pressing for attention, crises erupting frequently, and enormous pressure for rapid, accurate decision-making. The frustration that accompanies such roles can weigh heavily on the role's occupant.

The temptation to vent frustration in displays of temper in response can be irresistible. Though seemingly understandable, such displays negatively impact everyone around the executive with the most disastrous impact on the occupant themselves. Subordinates and colleagues quickly learn not to bring bad news for fear of triggering temper or being the object of same. Soon critical information is repressed, withheld, or downplayed in an effort to manage the executive's behavior out of fear. The effectiveness of the enterprise can be endangered. But perhaps most importantly, mature leadership doesn't display uncontrolled behavior, it is inappropriate, cruel and perhaps an actionable human resources issue.

Example: A University President was known to react with hostility, shouting, berating, and belittling

his executive team when unfortunate or unpleas-
ant results were communicated. The degree and
intensity of his temper response was unpredictable,
ranging from slight annoyance to an all-out scream-
ing fit. The fear engendered in the senior team made
members extremely reluctant to share bad news
until absolutely the last minute possible. Even then,
the team would frequently meet and "draw straws"
to see who would be the unlucky bearer of the bad
news, with their colleagues relieved – yet knowing full well that their moment in the victim's chair
would eventually come. The overwhelming dread
of cabinet meetings was palpable. Inevitably, critical information didn't flow to the top of the house
until an unprecedented crisis occurred, resulting
in Trustee scrutiny of the situation and consequent
undermining trust in the executive and a terminal
situation.

Another example. In another organization with
which we are familiar, an organization, faith-based
at that, a senior executive was installed who had a
well-known temper and short fuse. Frequently, in
meetings with subordinates, if something did not
meet his immediate approval, he would lash out at
these executives with expletive-laced invective completely inappropriate to the setting there or frankly
anywhere else. This behavior went on for several
years and had a very negative impact on the morale
of the senior executives – as you might expect.
However, as everyone was to find out, it may also
have had a negative impact on the abusive executive himself: He had a series of cardiac events which
ultimately (and thankfully to some) resulted in his
retirement with a medical disability. Another reason

to practice healthy leadership traits is to protect your own well-being, not just the well-being of your organization.

Displays of temper are a demonstration of lack of maturity, inability to manage one's behavior, and an automatic disqualifier for executive positions.

Vignette 11: Rip off the Bandage

Don't amputate by the inch: it's painful and yields poor, unfinished results

         – Informal medical school advice

Failed Essential Attribute	Honesty	Self-awareness	Emotional Maturity	Communicator	Decisiveness	Intelligence	Resilience
This vignette							

Hard decisions are just that, hard. But once the inevitable is apparent, the best and least costly path is usually straight-ahead decision implementation.

Senior executives face multiple instances of complex or even painful decision-making. Once sufficient information is gathered and analyzed and a course of action is planned, efficient implementation is the best course for an effective outcome.

Yet difficult decisions to terminate employees, exit unprom-ising businesses, or eschew unprofitable customers can lead senior executives to procrastinate, postpone, and repetitively analyze data sets in search of new revelations. The straight path from inevitable decision to best organizational outcome is most utilitarian yet still difficult.

> *Example:* A new CEO undertakes an operational review of the many corporate components report-ing to him. One executive supervising the flagship enterprise appears to be less than forthcoming in relating real-time data on operational outcomes. He is quite concerned about the inability to fully trust representations from the executive but chooses not

to disrupt his new "team" and just commits to paying close attention to the assurances emanating from that source.

After a rough patch of mixed signals and growing concern, the CEO learns, through secondary channels, that the flagship enterprise has sustained a "kiss of death" compliance result. The issue results in withdrawal of significant revenue from alarmed payors, negative publicity as local media highlight the noncompliance-causing incident, and negatively impacts customer confidence in other services of the parent organization.

He immediately removes the executive and institutes a complex turnaround plan and team, eventually succeeding in restoring compliance and operational effectiveness, but at significant revenue and reputational cost.

Following early judgment about the need to remove the executive would have been uncomfortable and stressful, but far less so than the end result.

Ripping off the bandage slowly causes more pain and inflammation than a quick stripping, but it is the path that even excellent leaders choose too often.

Vignette 12: Keep the Personal Away from the Professional

> All animals are equal, but some animals are more equal than others
>
> – George Orwell, *Animal Farm*

Failed Essential Attribute	Honesty	Self-awareness	Emotional Maturity	Communicator	Decisiveness	Intelligence	Resilience
This vignette							

Successful executives don't engage in inappropriate social or romantic relationships at work. They recognize and respect the difference between being friendly, being a friend, and expecting friendships "with benefits."

Unequal power can equal unequal treatment. Positions of executive authority or managerial responsibility carry power, whether realized and used or simply implied. Power over others and within organizations carries moral and frequently legal obligations. All too frequently, holders of leadership roles fail to maintain the boundaries of power that accompany those roles.

Close friendships and romantic relationships between leaders and other members of the company are always dangerous and frequently disastrous for individuals, careers, and organizations. Leadership positions impart power and authority. A close relationship with any individual reporting to the leader grants the leader power and authority over the friend or paramour. It also creates an unfair imbalance for others in the organization particularly when the relationship becomes known to others, and there is no such thing as an organizational secret. Whether the friend or paramour takes advantage of the relationship is immaterial.

> It should go without saying, but news stories rein-force the need for repetition: Successful executives don't engage in inappropriate social or romantic rela-tionships at work.
>
> There is no such thing as a level playing field or informed consent when one party's title begins with Chief or Senior VP and the other's begins with any-thing less in influence and power in the organization. It simply is exploitation, inappropriate, and down-right stupid to engage in a romantic or even close friendship with subordinates or colleagues in the work environment. It usually ends poorly since there is no such thing as an organizational secret when it comes to personal behavior. Don't do it, don't think it, and don't tolerate it from others.
>
> *Example.* Recently, as too often is the case, we provided interim executive support to an organiza-tion undergoing C-suite drama/trauma as the news that the CEO was having a romantic relationship with a subordinate emerged. Of course, this wasn't news to much of the organization's leadership, their flirta-tious behavior was obvious to everyone but them.
>
> When the Board received an anonymous whisper about the state of affairs, an investigation ensued. Details of inappropriate travel reimbursed by the company, padding of the budget for the subordinate's department, favoritism in decision-making, and even discomfort for support and administrative staff that were witness to the relationship all emerged. His career was over, she received a generous settlement after agreeing not to bring harassment litigation, and both marriages collapsed as did the original affair.

All leaders have power or authority over others. This creates an unequal relationship regardless of expressed assurances. Romantic relationships or even close personal friendships can negate the objectivity that should accompany executive decision-making. Unbalanced power gradients are inappropriate, frequently illegal, and always unwise. Keep the professional at work and the personal at home, always.

Vignette 13: Leader's Mind, But Not Brain, Is Lost

> Insanity is relative, it depends on who has who locked in what cage
>
> – Ray Bradbury

Failed Essential Attribute	Honesty	Self-awareness	Emotional Maturity	Communicator	Decisiveness	Intelligence	Resilience
This vignette							

In the course of a leadership career, you are certain to encounter someone who seems certifiably crazy. We use this term loosely and without professional psychiatric approval, but with knowledge that we all encounter "crazy people" and recognize the behavior when we meet them. The usual form of "nuts" is paranoia, a functioning sense that someone or a group of people are out to harm you, that trust cannot be extended without severe risk, and that one must be on guard against possible enemies at all times. Sometimes, this paranoia is twinned with a malignant narcissist personality – an unquenchable ego demanding that all must serve the leader, occasionally to the point that the organization is warped in service to the leader's warped psyche.

> We were asked to assist an organization in addressing extraordinarily high manager turnover in a complex healthcare organization. Analysis of the turnover yielded impactful data: The departing managers were frequently newly promoted young women. No one had noticed this vital clue to the source of management turmoil.

Closer scrutiny revealed that most of the departing managers reported through, or were tangentially influenced by, one senior officer of the company, the Chief Financial Officer. Interviews with departed managers revealed a pattern of blatant sexual harassment by the CFO. He had clearly linked continued organizational security with sexual favor expectations on numerous occasions. The situation was not only immoral, but it also presented significant legal and financial jeopardy to the company.

The CEO was presented with the accumulated data on the issue including the undeniable information on the behavior of the CFO. The CEO's response was unbelievable and caused the termination of the consultation. He thought that the contribution of the CFO to the organization far outweighed any issues with women subordinates, that he (the CEO) would not be able to function without the services of the CFO and that the entire issue was overblown. His absolute denial of reality led to the predictable disaster a few years later when the CFO's behavior resulted in the legal, financial, and publicity costs that accompany such dereliction of leadership responsibility.

The CFO had effectively bullied the CEO into accepting his perverse behavior out of the CEO's own fear of his self-perceived incompetence in financial matters. Both had lost their minds in pursuit of their personal goals: CFO's was power/harassment of subordinates, and CEO's was compensating for his self-perceived inadequacies.

Remarkably smart people can do remarkably stupid things if trapped in their own delusions.

Vignette 14: Family Business or Business of the Family?

> If you don't know where you're going any road will take you there
>
> – Lewis Carroll, *Alice in Wonderland*

Failed Essential Attribute	Honesty	Self-awareness	Emotional Maturity	Communicator	Decisiveness	Intelligence	Resilience
This vignette							

Many small businesses begin as a family enterprise. After the critical first three-year period, those surviving often continue to grow, but that growth may be suffocated by family priorities.

The business leader(s) must decide – once they are in a stable pattern – to remain small or continue to grow. Priorities must be set. Leadership cadres have to concur or it all will fall apart, as very likely will some of the family connections and priorities. It is quite difficult to balance family relationships with business decisions when the two are intertwined. In order for necessary changes to be accepted, decisions must be made about where to draw prioritization lines between what is family and what is business.

> *Example:* In a consultation with a manufacturing and regional distribution company located at a time-zone boundary, dozens of significant recommendations were accepted, implemented, and company gains were celebrated with a large extended family function over a weekend.
>
> Problem? One more revenue-significant recommendation was to change a particular function by

an hour, so as to be able to take advantage of an earlier shipping time and beat the competition across the time zone. That interfered with a golf tee time of one of the owners, who wanted to be on hand for that process. Focus and prioritization within the family couldn't be sorted, and the decision emerged to maintain current process so as not to disrupt the owner's social schedule. The resultant difference was foregoing a significant competitive advantage and revenue contribution, all because family ties were more influential than achieving pragmatic financial outcomes. The difference could have been a 20–30% revenue gain with essentially no additional costs.

Although not directly a negative business outcome, such behaviors not only could strongly influence business outcomes, but also they may profoundly impact family–domestic relationships resulting from business opportunities missed or downturns. "Face" is more important than often considered, and its challenges may be deeply insidious and recognized only too late – both for business and for domestic relations.

Choose and then knowingly prioritize: family or business – cannot both be highest priority! There are many valid reasons for wanting a business or institution to remain modest; however, clarity around that decision should be understood, rather than remaining implicit – many careers or futures may hinge on it. Choices may be optional.

Vignette 15: Bureaucratic Success, Mission Leadership Failure

> Bureaucracy is the art of making the possible impossible
> – Javier Pascual Salcedo

Failed Essential Attribute	Honesty	Self-awareness	Emotional Maturity	Communicator	Decisiveness	Intelligence	Resilience
This vignette							

Many of us are called to leadership roles in bureaucracies.

Organizations can be defined as bureaucracies when they are layered with levels of decision-making, complex rules, processes, and systems all focused on maintaining control. Though the typical bureaucracy is a government entity, it is quite possible to encounter this structure in a large non-profit entity or even some corporate structures.

It is possible, though challenging, to be an effective leader in a bureaucracy. But it requires more than the usual abilities to communicate, motivate and make decisions.

We encountered a state-sponsored bureaucracy where the C-suite executives had attained and maintained position through excellence at working the cumbersome processes, negotiating frequently nonsensical rules, and pleasing "superiors" in the state oversight function. They became so adept at working the bureaucratic system that they lost site of the organization's core mission of behavioral health patient care. Frontline staff morale, effectiveness, and soon basic decency eroded over time. As managers focused on maintaining good relationships with distant bureaucratic superiors and complying with myriad rules and processes, a litany of care and safety risks accrued. Finally, a tragic incident leading to patient harm (death!) occurred. An external regulatory audit revealed a broken system unable to deliver even the most basic of care as mandated by the system's mission. Revocation of licensure and closure was threatened until a complete institutional turnaround was achieved.

A deep-dive assessment revealed a leadership structure focused on pleasing state oversight authorities with little to no contact with the actual business of caring for patients.

The CEO was so disengaged from the mission that he couldn't lead a tour of the grounds. He was completely detached from the actual service environment. He had been considered a successful leader because all paperwork was submitted in a timely fashion, personnel functions were without grievance, budget allocations were scrupulously managed, and superiors were kept blithely unaware of the state of mayhem at the point of service. Leaders had mastered the art of bureaucracy and totally failed the obligation to the core mission.

It is possible to be both an effective leader and successful bureaucrat, it simply means balancing the requirements of the systems and processes required by the bureaucracy with a continued eye on the mission, your purpose for joining the organization. Fortunately, we have many leaders who successfully achieve this duality of purpose to give us effective government and other complex organizations layered with bureaucracy.

Vignette 16: Leadership Failure Cascade

> The greater the power, the more dangerous the abuse.
> – Edmund Burke

Failed Essential Attribute	Honesty	Self-awareness	Emotional Maturity	Communicator	Decisiveness	Intelligence	Resilience
This vignette							

Leadership failure is frequently viewed as an individual event, perhaps a professional disaster for the leader involved, but still a relatively isolated incident. This view is far from reality.

When a leader fails, the organization suffers. If the failure is sudden such as the leader publicly humiliated because of a personal transgression (think a DUI arrest making the local paper), the impact might be less significant, though some loss of leadership is still impactful, regardless. If the leadership failure is due to deficits in leadership attributes such as indecisiveness or displays of temper, the organizational impact can be huge and might even lead to organizational failure. We term this a Leadership Failure Cascade: Setting the organization on a path to repeat failure at multiple levels.

It is a slippery slope going from minor slights – leader being late to meetings, keeping cellphones and fingers on electronic screens during others' presentations, and the like – to the larger cascade of failures suggested above. Rudeness and lacking respect easily slip first to minor, then later, to major institutional failures.

A very prosperous private investment management firm with decades of successive growth was stumbling. Assets under management (a key measure of success) were stagnant. New client acquisition was glacial and old clients began to exit the firm due to dissatisfaction with service efficiency and effectiveness. The Management Committee spent hours analyzing data, scrutinizing performance indicators and anecdotal evidence from former clients' customer evaluations. Every indicator evaluated was middling to declining. Yet no one seemed to grasp what actions to take.

A consultant was engaged to evaluate the situation. One-on-one interviews yielded uniform results: the managing partners and senior principals all regarded the current Chief Operating Officer as incompetent to the task. He dithered at decision-making, couldn't develop or lead administrative staff, implementation of information technology lagged well behind announced deadlines, and promising new personnel left the firm with rapidity. When the consultant's summary was presented to the Management Committee there was uniform agreement with the validity of conclusions. Yet there was also a hesitancy to take action; all had known the COO for years; he had been promoted to the role after acceptable service in a management role and was a good friend of the recently retired Board chair.

The five-person committee was loath to initiate change, but also unwilling to accept the status quo. These two mutually exclusive results were obviously incompatible. Yet no one seemed able to move toward resolution. Finally, the consultant offered to "have the Talk" with the COO: In essence giving him performance feedback based on the assessment. The need to engage an outsider to execute a critical decision seemed to finally move the Management Committee (MC) to action.

The COO was provided with the feedback report prior to meeting with the MC. At the meeting, he expressed relief that the situation was coming to a resolution; he had realized that operations were flagging, didn't know what to do, and welcomed being removed from the COO role!

The impact of the COO's poor performance became acutely visible after his departure. Midmanagers sought better definition of their roles and responsibilities. Line staff sought clarification of processes. New systems and services were quickly implemented. The organizational impact, the leadership failure cascade, became evident.

A subsequent management reorganization coupled with a renewed dedication to excellence in client service revivified the firm. It regained several key lost clients, grew assets under management, and continues to prosper.

In hindsight, the leadership failure cascade at the investment firm was readily apparent.

The art of leadership includes the ability to perceive organizational trends and changes in real time. Noting that one manager is not a good fit might be the first step, but recognizing the systemic impact of a poor leader is only a prerequisite to the action that needs to be taken. It is interesting to note that after a necessary leadership transition many folks will comment "I knew he couldn't make it." Yet few folks have the ability to identify much less the courage to take action in prevention.

Personal service can be honored and action required can be taken, but the mission also needs to be respected – both for the institution and individuals' careers.

Vignette 17: Boards Bruise the Business

Be careful what you ask for

– Judicial Commentary

Failed Essential Attribute	Honesty	Self-awareness	Emotional Maturity	Communicator	Decisiveness	Intelligence	Resilience
This vignette							

Boards have vast authority, literally representing the interests of the shareholders.

The best Boards comprehend that their authority should be restricted to setting mission, affirming vision, providing fiduciary oversight, hiring, advising, evaluating the CEO, and, when required, terminating the CEO. That is a large portfolio for what essentially is a lofty but part-time job. Truly excellent companies recruit, orient, and support Boards that stick to this role. Wandering outside of these boundaries frequently leads to disaster. Excellent CEO leaders spend significant time managing Board relations, expectations, and helping the Board "stay in their lane." Truly great CEOs welcome an inquisitive (not intrusive) Board: Asking good questions.

> A large manufacturing association is named in litigation as one of many responding parties, including companies that are members of the association. The association's CEO and attorneys duly inform the Board and keep its members abreast of activities even though the attorneys, Board, and management believe that the association is inappropriately named and is later dropped from the suit as another responsible party settles the case. You would think that life would return to "status quo ante," but no.

Several members of the Board are not satisfied with the legal outcome of explicitly not being held responsible and seek further litigation, even though the association has been eliminated from the suit. The association's CEO and attorneys forcefully advise otherwise, urge all to be satisfied with the outcome: Move back to the business of the business is their advice. The dominant Board members (who coincidentally work for association members) disagree and direct the attorneys to pursue new litigation against the original complainant.

A jury trial is requested. Not only does the jury not find for the association, but the jury views the litigation as unfounded and awards significant damages ($49 million!) to the original complainant.

Members of the association are livid at the Board's decision to pursue litigation against the advice of legal counsel. They in turn sue the individual Board members for recovery of the awarded damages. The legal findings agree with the association members, and Board members were found to have acted against the interests of the association and are thus directed to personally compensate the association for their $49 million award in damages.

Another example of Board negligence follows.
Boards represent the "owners" of the organization, whether shareholders, investors, or – in the case of non-profit organizations – the community and clients served. Boards that fail to recall their role as representatives of the "owners" can lead the organization into deep peril and even closure. The role of the Board is to keep a keen eye on the mission of the organization, to hire, guide, and replace as necessary

the senior leader(s) of the organization when they
fail to serve the mission appropriately. The failure to
recall why the organization exists, its mission, has
led many Boards into deep peril.

One hospital with which we were asked to work
vividly represents this Board mission attention failure.
This public institution has performed well financially,
growing volume and expanding business. The Board
had even overseen the establishment of a lovely
community recreation center by the hospital as an
additional community service. While focused on the
robust financial position of the hospital, on reaching
out in the community for other services, and on the
many accolades the hospital leader had accumulated
for his exemplary service, the Board failed to attend
to its actual purpose, safeguarding the mission of the
hospital: simply delivering safe patient care.

Physicians and nursing staff became increasingly
concerned about lapses in patient care delivery due
to outdated equipment, insufficient clinical supplies, and a lack of continuing attention to training and education in new care delivery methods.
Incidences of patient harm became more frequent
and were of particular concern to physicians staffing
the Emergency Department. After several attempts
to bring these incidences to the attention of the CEO
without success, one physician addressed concerns in
a detailed letter to the Board. The physician was terminated from her position through the CEO's efforts
in response.

The physician, with encouragement from colleagues, brought the issues of lapses in care quality
to the State Health regulatory authority. They initiated
an unannounced inspection, validated the concerns,

and reported the hospital to federal authorities. A second and third inspection culminated in the hospital's termination from federal funding (Medicare and Medicaid), a result that terminates private insurance funding. This effectively chokes off the vast majority of financial support and predictably results in hospital closure.

The core issue that almost closed this community resource was the Board's failure to stay close to the mission. They had become so enraptured by the siren call of expansion, diversification, and general community image, that the basic assurance of safe hospital care was lost as a Board obligation. Only the investment of significant resources in the implementation of a successful corrective action plan saved the hospital from closure.

Message: Boards need to stick to the knitting. What is the core mission of the company? How well do we serve that mission? How can we improve that service?

The role of the Board is phenomenally important, the Board can make or break the business. But like all critical leadership functions, Boards need to comprehend and abide by their role and responsibility. It is particularly important for individual Board members to leave their ego, agenda, and feelings in the background and bring clear-eyed leadership to bear on their tasks.

Vignette 18: Don't Confuse Activity with Productivity

> Nothing is less productive than to make more efficient that which should not be done at all
>
> — Peter Drucker

Failed Essential Attribute	Honesty	Self-awareness	Emotional Maturity	Communicator	Decisiveness	Intelligence	Resilience
This vignette							

Organizations are purpose-built, designed to deliver the results obtained. If functioning well, competently led, and staffed appropriately, good results will follow. But some organizations get caught up in a frenzy of activity mistaking busyness for output and motion for progress. The organizational message becomes "look busy," "do something, anything."

> *Example*: A midwestern regional health system was managing to stay slightly ahead of creditors, deliver acceptable health care, and attract competent staff. Yet, though it was the sole provider of services in many of its communities, it couldn't seem to really prosper. The CEO, an experienced executive, couldn't understand the lack of progress, the inability to ever attain stretch goals or engage in innovation. In his frustration, he engaged a renowned consulting group led by a charismatic senior member.
>
> The initial organizational assessment was that the system needed a new aspirational plan to excel. The consulting firm proposed, and the CEO accepted,

an ambitious customer service program designed to impact every level and function of the system. New management responsibilities for coaching and evaluating subordinates were implemented. Continuous management attention to customer feedback was required. Thousands of hours-of-service training were conducted. Banners, badges, and billboards festooned the campuses with proclamations of patient first expectations.

At the close of the 18-month launch, the CEO evaluated selected metrics and was disturbed that after a significant investment in staff time, consulting fees, and executive attention, metrics reflected a further decline in customer satisfaction, clinical quality outcome measures, and erosion of financial performance. Yet everyone was incredibly busy. Managers and Directors attended hours of meetings each day then conducted staff rounds to meet and greet front-line employees and deliver scripted comments about performance prior to filling out reems of paperwork to document myriad Patient First responsibilities.

Where was the missed connection? The senior leader had mistaken activity for productivity. Instead of a deep dive into the organization to assess alignment and directionality, the CEO had inflicted an additional time-consuming responsibility on a system that was already limping along. Thousands of hours and millions of dollars invested yielded declining results.

W. Edwards Deming famously said: "People with targets and jobs dependent upon meeting them will probably meet the targets-even if they have to destroy the enterprise to do it."

Even when conscientiously carrying out the CEO's role – adhering to mission, function, staffing, and finances as set out by a Board – measuring same requires insight to distinguish activity from results. Insanity is defined by some as having an expectation that same actions repeated will bring different results. Sanity for the institution requires the CEO to act on metrics and trends, to morph from activity without purpose to targeted productivity when needed. Static management (not the same as stable management) is a harbinger of coming demise.

Vignette 19: Small Intervention But Huge Impact

> For want of a nail the shoe was lost,
> For want of a shoe the horse was lost;
> And for want of a horse the rider was lost;
> Being overtaken and slain by the enemy,
> All for want of care about a horseshoe-nail.
>   – Benjamin Franklin's 1758 *The Way to Wealth*

Failed Essential Attribute	Honesty	Self-awareness	Emotional Maturity	Communicator	Decisiveness	Intelligence	Resilience
This vignette							

In many organizations, there are impediments that creep into view like a dripping faucet: slowly and with time very destructively. The maximum leader or a major player (rainmaker, fund-raiser, public-relations maven, innovation leader) slowly creeps beyond acceptable bounds and has no trusted insider to check the behaviors that could ruin the reputation, lose the business, or end up killing the enterprise. The great leadership failure here is not addressing the issue at first sighting. The earlier it is caught, the smaller the likely growing list of unintended consequences.

Examples are many. Here are just a few.

A half-day retreat costing a few thousand dollars very likely saved more than millions of dollars in litigation and potential settlements. By cloaking a problem within the context of performing a SWOTA (Strengths, Weaknesses, Opportunities, Threats Analysis) with an entire leadership cadre, our

consulting team was able to redirect a leader's ener-
gies and preclude further inappropriate gender-based
"benign" harassment. Instead of a public-relations
disaster, the company went on a growth spree.

Another Board did not know how to confront a
CEO with a pattern of activities that – together with
a public-figure spouse – involved increasingly and
very public alcoholic consumption that risked public
embarrassment for the organization. The issue was
broader, because not only were others on the Board
and in one-down leadership roles afraid or unable
to confront the CEO, but for several, the "well-fueled
festive activities" were perceived as entertaining and
"fun." Avoiding a profound public disaster took a private conversation from the consultant that was understood by the CEO who changed behavior. A simple
straightforward conversation saved his position.

Even now, in the broadened computer age, one
finds CEOs whose knowledge of either some part
of the institutional mission or an important support
function required for mission success is minimal.
In an open environment: no problem. In an ego-
blocked environment, "face" gets in the way. This
can be as simple as not understanding the numbers
(finances; production; impact analyses) or general
information technology – thus allowing a subordinate freedom to "game" a system to the detriment
of the system and possibly for great personal gain.
Or it may result in a stubbornness borne out of a
reluctance to back off a run of bad decisions and
seek assistance. In a rather public instance, an entire
and historically significant service subject to national
accreditation and compliance requirements in one
hospital lost its ability – along with many millions of
dollars in revenue – to continue offering a significant

service. It took many months following a leadership change to rebuild an acceptable capacity and again provide that important service for the larger community. For reasons of priority among many other ongoing changes, the consulting recommendations had been heard for a quick change (cheap at the price), but could not be acted upon until the service was suspended – accompanied by a very significant revenue loss. This important service for the public was able to be re-established, but only after rather detrimental downtime.

Small but external impactful interventions may be the only way to make "save the bacon" changes.

Vignette 20: The No-Bell Prize

Cheap at Twice the Price; Also, never try to quietly out-guess or undercut the owners or Board
— Our "No-Bell Prize" Committee

Failed Essential Attribute	Honesty	Self-awareness	Emotional Maturity	Communicator	Decisiveness	Intelligence	Resilience
This vignette							

Leaders frequently miss detecting tactical blunders or significant opportunities within their organization when they delegate but neglect to verify.

This is not at odds with the importance of trusting managers and staff, and even encouraging "tinkering" where not inconsistent with the organizational mission. Leadership includes a mentoring ability that allows for attempts at improvement to fail; it does not, however, negate the importance of verifying results.

For example, in one facility where the corporate culture encouraged feedback and improvements, something didn't seem to be right.

Repeated attempts to attend to budget created a misalignment between form and substance or between top and mid-level management. It took a personal walk-through by a Board member to discover – and quickly remedy – the issue.

What had happened? In order to save on personnel, jobs were coalesced to save one FTE. Repeated community feedback was showing a reduction in service in one area; hence, revenues were falling for that service.

As is often true in larger organizations, frontline staff in this case did personally not recognize the Board member, who appeared to be "just someone" at the time of the personal walk-through to do the deep dive to try to discover the problem.

After several face-to-face attempts to get the data to determine the cause leading to the undesired effect, the questioner was directed to go to the office now reduced by an FTE, a result of shared responsibilities with another department. The office had a sign on the window intended to cover the circumstance when no one was visible in the working area. The sign? *RING BELL FOR HELP.*

All good. Or maybe not. The problem: there was no bell!

In another example, a CEO who had been promoted beyond capabilities made a serious error in judgment, hoping to have a "looking good" budgetary outcome.

A very creative business owner came up with an innovative solution to jump ahead of the competition and solve an industry problem. The path to get there involved a large expenditure in equipment, its customization, and the development of plans for scheduling installation and successful implementation. When reviewing the checklist with the CEO of requirements shortly before installation of the final product was due to occur, the owner learned that heavy-duty, expensive, wiring and electrical installation had not been completed on schedule; in fact, it had not even been started. A very costly delay.

What had happened (or not happened)? The CEO had decided not to spend the projected less than a hundred thousand dollars to get the preparations in order.

Going against the owner's wishes! Saving tens of thousands of dollars after an expenditure of hundreds of thousands of dollars! Halting projected progress!

You can accurately guess the follow-up remedies for these stories. (Yes, after the personnel "fixes," service, production, and revenues for the Departments in question improved.)

When in business, Remember: "We are in business to make money, not to save money"

Chapter 2

Essentials for Success

> Your assumptions are your windows on the world. Scrub
> them off once in a while, or the light won't come in
>   – Isaac Asimov

Leaders come in many packages. There is no gender, race,
ethnic, personality type, or age requirement for the role.
Women lead in the military, men lead in nursing, young entre-
preneurs grow successful companies, old leaders reinvent their
roles in new organizations. The stereotypical image of the
take-charge CEO as a white, middle-aged male just doesn't (or
shouldn't) apply as a requirement in the contemporary world
of business.

But regardless of demographic descriptors, there are essential attributes that do characterize successful leaders across
business and organizational types. We have identified seven
attributes that are integral components of a leader and the
absence of which can trigger a leadership failure:

1. Honesty/integrity
2. Self-awareness

DOI: 10.4324/9781003304371-4

3. Emotional maturity
4. Communicator
5. Decisiveness
6. Intelligence
7. Resilience

The literature is replete with deep studies of organizations, quality work, and leadership. Our conclusions, unlike the work of such luminaries as Blanchard, Block, Collins, Covey, Deming, Goldschmidt, Greenleaf, Juran, Kotter, Rubenstein,* and many others popularized during the past several decades, are based on neither formal studies nor paradigmatic pathways disseminated and implemented by consultants, rather on our experiential base. Our descriptors focus on the opposite of success factors.

Rather, we look backward at both a balance among attributes and those which when missing have yielded failures. Thus, our focus is on avoiding or fixing failures, not on growing successes. The difference is subtle. The attributes discussed in the following section do not stand alone. There is, perforce, considerable overlap and interaction among them in real leadership environments. A key concept, as noted above, is worth repeating: It is about balance, rather than checking off boxes on a "to-do" list.

Given the work we have done – more at organizations in serious trouble and some at the very top of what they do than those in the middle of the pack – we have acquired a different view…both about organizations and their individual leaders.

In the end, whether drawing statistics on quality outcomes, servant leadership goals, financial results, or whatever, there

---

* Rubenstein, David M., 2020.

is much common ground. The difference in our sights has been to help leaders get there without relying on yet one more expensive initiative or heavy-budgeted lengthy study. Perhaps best said by Nike's adage: "just do it."

One admonition: When "just doing it," do measure results, gather and track trends, and keep doing that, and never lose sight that trust, as a central ingredient allows, nay requires, constructive criticisms and openness to same in all directions.

A few key questions prepare the reader to be able to use this content for a guide. Thus, we've added some questions to the end of each attribute section to help evaluate your leadership role in terms of your own career and in terms of the institution where you are or wish to be located.

> Significant and successful leadership actions most often are situational, rather than formulaic. Outcomes need to be tracked. Adjustments need to be made in response. Standing firm on bad decisions cannot serve the organization or the leader well.

Attribute 1: Honesty/Integrity

Be true not only unto yourself, but also
to your organization

– Anonymous

The attribute of honesty would seem a "no brainer" as critical
to leadership success. Who would trust, much less follow, a
liar? Yet contemporary society is abundantly demonstrative of
successful liars. Our experience demonstrates the eventual failure of these characters, though some do seem to succeed for
a good run. Trust is the currency of effectiveness and, to state
the obvious, there is no trust once dishonesty is apparent.
Additionally, the energy consumed in maintaining a façade or
charade in the presence of dishonest pronouncements can be
significant. As grandmother said, "While you can always trust
a thief, you can never trust a liar." Sage advice.

There is an additional measure to integrity that should not
be overlooked: Convergence of personal and institutional
philosophies. Being efficient, effective, and not cheating are
all requisites for good leadership; sustaining good practices
and on-target delivery of mission mostly is also dependent on
avoiding conflicts between or among personal practices and
beliefs and those core to an institution or organization. Too
many examples of this mismatch show up very publicly in
political realms, where – perhaps – a rule of "do what I say,
not what I do" undercuts the best of intentions. For example,
a corporation of some prominence launched a much-heralded
diversity initiative to assure that personnel reflected the communities of consumers served, a diverse representation of race,
gender, socioeconomic level, ability, and religion. Yet after
the first years of implementation, it was apparent to all who
looked that the dozen occupants of senior leadership were

entirely white and, with the exception of one lone woman, male. Again, "do as I say and not as I do" appears to be the prevailing mantra.

It is, however, worth mentioning here that there are boundaries around full disclosure: It is not the same as transparency. Diplomatic transparency beats cruel honesty. When out of phase, you perceive cognitive dissonance, and that is not helpful. As a base image, for example, would you really want to see your Board in action totally naked?

Personal Leadership Questions (Honesty/Integrity)

- Am I on a "slippery slope"? What sort of ethics shortcuts do I take in my business practices?
- Who do I use to "check my thinking" to be sure I am processing clearly and honestly?
- How rigorous is the use of third parties to be sure business practices are "above board"?

Institutional Leadership Questions (Honesty/Integrity)

- Are you, your Board, and other Leadership in synch and behaving solely within ethical bounds with focus on the institutional mission success rather than any individual and personal gains?
- If there are exceptions to the above, are you able to call them out, or do you put up with them – and if so, how comfortable are you with your lack of fit in that situation?

Integrity is the individual's keystone partner to the organization's mission. Absent both, success cannot linger long.

Attribute 2: Self-Awareness

> O wad some pow'r the giftie gie us to see oursels
> as ithers see us
> (*Burns wishes for the power to see ourselves as others see us*)
> – Robert Burns

At its most basic, self-awareness is being able to recognize your emotions and feelings and how these affect your thoughts, which in turn impacts your behavior.

As a leader your actions impact others. Self-awareness in the context we use it is about having insight into how others perceive you in an organizational context based on those actions. How do those you lead perceive you as their leader – are you perceived as "tough but fair," as a "pushover," as someone who plays favorites, or some other behavioral set of attributes?

What makes self-awareness so challenging is that it isn't just a one-directional phenomenon. We also project how we want to be perceived by others. Thus, a component of being self-aware is being intentional about how you want to be perceived by those in your organization. If you want to be seen as someone who is kind and compassionate, what do you do that others see to make them reach that conclusion? If you want to be perceived as competent and efficient, how do you model that behavior to those you lead?

The leaders we have seen who have some mastery of self-awareness really work at it. To develop self-awareness, leaders need multiple feedback loops – both formal and informal. Many organizations help leaders in the quest to become more self-aware by providing access to various personality inventories, work-style assessments, and other diagnostic tools for self-reflection. These can be very helpful to gain insight into what are your key emotional drivers to cause you to act a certain way.

In addition, the higher your position in the organization, the more important it is to cultivate multiple avenues of feedback about how your actions are impacting those you lead. It is unfortunate, but for obvious reasons nevertheless a reality, that many people subordinate to you won't give unvarnished feedback.

A leader serious about being truly self-aware will welcome honest, direct feedback. It may also be helpful to engage the services of a management coach – someone whose job it is to give you the kind of honest, constructive feedback that can help you gain a better understanding of how you can positively impact the health of your organization by your actions.

Personal Leadership Questions (Self-Awareness)

- Can I accept criticisms constructively? Do I invite them?
- Am I able to be fair? Do I understand that identical reactions are not always better than equivalent but fair actions?
- Is respect mutual among your subordinates, superiors, and yourself?
- Do I have a thought partner (coach or external consultant) who can assist me in this assessment?

Institutional Leadership Questions (Self-Awareness)

- Can you praise subordinates publicly and engage them privately when corrections are needed?
- Are you aware when outside help is needed, and does the institution support that external energy when it is needed?

Failure to understand how you are perceived can lead to misunderstanding and misperceptions. Having an "honest broker" who can give you unvarnished feedback is essential to leadership.

Attribute 3: Emotional Maturity

> Being an adult is mostly going to bed when you don't
> want to and waking up when you don't want to
> — Anonymous

The ability to step outside of the situation and perceive impact, but also the ability to manage impact on oneself – these form the core of emotional maturity.

There will be challenges, even defeats. The emotionally mature leader manages both in stride, accepts reality, and doesn't see challenge as a personal affront to one's own being. Managing emotions and behavioral responses to difficult or even wildly successful events allows a leader not to be manipulated by external forces or people. This attribute may be termed "acting like an adult."

Adults are able to recognize a reality that includes their role and responsibilities in an organization. They are also able to accept and seek compensatory mechanisms to address their own limitations. When confronted with errors, particularly of their own making, adults can accept responsibility, acknowledge the issue, and seek corrective action. The phrase: "I messed up and I'm sorry" may be difficult to voice, but can garner great respect and reinforce transparency and openness as an organizational virtue.

Hiding mistakes is for children and criminals. The emotionally mature leader is able to recognize her own limits, set boundaries, and ask for assistance when needed. She also understands the impact of stress, tension, and pressure on optimal functioning and seeks respite when her limits of tolerance are being reached.

The emotionally mature leader understands that life is a journey. Leaders constantly seek to renew their skills, hone their abilities, and master new information. Bringing the same solutions and answers to each challenge solves little. Growth and learning are never-ending quests. No one is finished until the end is reached.

Too few leaders are able to receive effective feedback about performance, opportunities for improvement, or issues of style from within their own organizations. The dynamics of organizational power preclude candid feedback in the vast majority of situations. Emotionally mature leaders understand the need to continually grow and evolve and seek information to assist or guide this journey. This may be the best use of an outside consultant as a leadership coach, honest partner, and professional friend able to give candid and straightforward input without positional threat or fear.

Personal Leadership Questions (Emotional Maturity)

- Do I hire for emotional intelligence?
- How do I get feedback about my own emotional maturity?

Institutional Leadership Questions (Emotional Maturity)

- What is the emotional intelligence of my team?
- How does the organization react to urgent or crisis situations?
- Are people rewarded for identifying problems or mistakes?

Emotionally mature leaders will strongly consider using an external advisor to help them become better leaders.

Attribute 4: Communicator

> The single biggest problem with communication is the illusion that it has taken place
>
> – George Bernard Shaw

It has been said that a key role of the chief executive officer is "chief sense-maker." That is, the CEO is tasked with taking in all kinds of external and internal data, synthesizing it, communicating what it means in the organization, and then developing plans for how the organization responds. This is true of any leader in the organization – no matter their level. This means taking external and internal inputs and translating them so the people you lead can understand and use them to guide their priorities and actions in order to achieve the organizational results desired.

Making sense of complex, even conflicting information is a big challenge. It might be an even bigger challenge communicating what message to take from all of those inputs throughout the organization.

It is obvious that all leaders need to be able to communicate effectively with those they lead. But if it is so obvious and everyone needs to do it, why is it so hard to do effectively? In fact, in a simple Google review of the top reasons why leaders fail, lack of effective communication is always high on the list.

When most people in business or other organizations hear the word "communication," they likely think talking, memos, posters, or some other form of messaging where the message is delivered to the intended audience through multiple forms of media. This is a valid and important part of the communication loop. But it is incomplete.

What this overlooks, of course, is active listening as a form of communication. It takes at least two to complete a communication loop: One is issuing the message and the other is receiving it. We are familiar with too many executives who fail to understand the role of active listening as a part of effective communication.

Let's take a closer look at how a leader can be a more effective communicator in an organization.

By the very title of "leader," that person most likely has many audiences with whom to communicate. All leaders have a boss or bosses to whom they report. Every leader – by definition – has people to lead.

Leaders might also have groups of people outside the organization with whom they need to communicate, such as shareholders, advisory boards, governmental agencies, community organizations, and the like. An explicit understanding of your audience is essential to developing an effective plan of communication. Who are your audiences and how are they best communicated with?

Once you know who your audiences are, you need to appreciate how each group best consumes communication from you: Is it by memo, PowerPoint, or in-person oral communication? Your messages are only as effective as the ability of the audience to receive them. So make it a point to know how each audience prefers to receive your communication and deliver it to them that way.

In this age where social media plays such an integral part in how people communicate with each other, it is important to understand how appropriate use of social media can help you communicate with your constituencies. The role of social media is a fast-changing target, and you must surround yourself with people who understand and live in that reality and can apply it to your business needs, helping you navigate how to use social media and which platforms are best suited to your industry and messaging needs.

What are your particular communication strengths? Are you a good writer? If not, find a writer/editor to help. Are you good at making oral presentations standing in front of groups of people? If not, take an oral presentations course, such as Toastmasters International.

A plan of communication needs to be a part of every significant decision in your organization. This should not be left to the end, as an afterthought, and then be patched together. Integrate the communication plan into the decision-making process: Make it an essential part of how the organization does business.

How do you take in information from your constituencies... what are your key listening posts? Do you read customer-feedback reports, attend focus groups, respond directly to customer complaints? How do you get employee input and feedback? Do you schedule time to meet with key constituencies in order to just listen to what their issues are and get feedback on how things are going?

Although there is some "art" in the ability to be an effective communicator, there is more "science." A leader doesn't need to be a great orator or writer to be effective, but you do need to know your audiences and how they can best receive your message. In summary, the steps to being an effective communicator are as follows:

a. Know who your audiences are – every leader has multiple audiences – who are they?
b. Determine how each audience prefers to be communicated.
c. With written, oral, in-person, video – often it will be a combination.
d. How often do you need to communicate with each audience?
e. Know your own preferred style of communication and augment your weaknesses with help from others.

f. How effective of a listener are you...how do you take in feedback from the organization? Can you sit and listen to others without formulating your response first?
g. Make communication plans an integral part of every decision you make in the organization?

Personal Leadership Questions (Communicator)

■ Do you follow the advice relating to having two ears and one mouth?
■ Do you understand the strength of aligning your communication strategies with the needs of your audiences?

Institutional Leadership Questions (Communicator)

■ Are there communication plans for your major institutional decisions?
■ Can you use external feedback to improve decision-making and attain desired results?

Great communicators are made not born – it takes effort, energy and humility to become an effective communicator.

Attribute 5: Decisiveness

Not to decide is to decide
— An old piece of management wisdom

A key factor of successful leadership is the ability to make consistently good decisions in a timely and effective manner. This sounds simple and straightforward enough, yet it is remarkable in our experience to see how many leaders fail because they can't be decisive enough or, on the other hand, make monstrously poor decisions that threaten their careers as well as the security of their organizations.

To be fair, decision-making in the business environment isn't easy. In large organizations, there are often bureaucratic layers defining how decisions are made, but that may or may not be well articulated. The executive is left to navigate this complexity and "feel" her way around to avoid stepping on toes or worse, being tagged with a decision that failed. Failure in the corporate environment is often punished despite senior executives' protests to the contrary.

In recent years, with the vibrant new business start-up environment brought about in part by discoveries in digital technology, much has been written about rapid iterating which requires quick decision-making, oftentimes failure, learning from that failure, then iterating a new solution until you get it right. These environments tolerate and even reward failure as long as you are learning and failing forward.

Depending on what kind of environment you are working in, your decision-making style will have to match. That said, there are some basic structures to good decisions that apply in any workplace.

A decision-making framework

Most good decisions that aren't the result of chance or luck have certain fundamental traits.

a. The problem to be solved has been well defined and well understood by the decision maker(s).
b. What results you are expecting by way of improvement once the decision is implemented are anticipated and able to be measured.
c. A plan for how you will make adjustments (iterative process) in the likelihood you didn't get it 100% right at first.

Common failures in good decision-making include analysis paralysis, authoritarian (my way or the highway) leadership style, and reluctance/inability to pivot to another solution once it becomes clear the decision made isn't solving the problem.

There are many explanations why executives get stuck analyzing a problem to death and avoid being decisive. The cultural norms for decision-making in an organization may reward a CYA approach where you get multiple sign-offs before making a decision as a way of dispersing blame if you get it wrong.

In our experience, we see failure to be decisive while analyzing a situation endlessly often interferes with personnel decisions. Decisions about people such as where they fit organizationally, whether they are doing a good job or not, or whether they need to exit the organization are necessarily difficult to make. Delays in making difficult personnel decisions though can have significant negative impact on the organization. Using the framework described above can help expedite making those decisions and avoiding unnecessary organizational harm.

The authoritarian decision maker uses positional authority and/or subject-matter expertise to impose a solution on the organization. There are times such as an acute crisis when this style of decision-making can be useful. However, most of the time, this style of leadership thwarts participation and stifles the creativity of team members. This is a particularly malignant style of leadership because it can be dangerous to challenge this person openly and unless other senior leaders act, it can be difficult to get this person to adjust their style.

The third way decisions fail is a result of not being rigorous enough in applying the decision-making process. If the executive or team haven't sufficiently defined what a successful decision looks like in objective terms, a suboptimal result could be allowed to linger much longer than is healthy for the organization. If the executive or management team invested a lot of sweat equity into a solution, their emotional attachment may obscure for them what would be necessary to best alter the decision (iterate) or change course altogether. It is critical to have objective data to evaluate the effectiveness of key decisions in order to evaluate the success of the solution and make changes as needed to adjust the solution.

Personal Leadership Questions (Decisiveness)

- What is my preferred decision-making process?
- How effective is it?
- How do I "check my thinking" when making decisions?

Institutional Leadership Questions (Decisiveness)

- How does my decision-making process fit in my organization?
- Do my colleagues feel safe offering contrarian perspectives? How do I know that?

Successful leaders will understand their decision-making style, adjust it to the norms of the organization, and be rigorous in defining what success looks like.

Attribute 6: Intelligence

> Intelligence is like underwear: it's important that you have
> it, but not necessarily that you show it off...
> — Anonymous

A key characteristic of good leadership is intelligence. This
may not be as obvious as it sounds.

A quick review of relevant popular literature will reveal
many types of intelligence. These include logical-mathematical,
linguistic, spatial, musical, kinesthetic, intrapersonal, interper-
sonal, naturalistic, among many others.

Certainly, a leader in a complex organizational environment
would need to be "intelligent" in many of these categories. A
leader needs to have a facility with numbers in order to read
or produce, and certainly to analyze, financial and other sta-
tistical reports. Leaders also need to have the ability to relate
well to others and have a good sense of themselves – what
has been described by others as "emotional intelligence." The
leader needs to be able to communicate effectively and thus
needs to be "intelligent" in the use of language for writing and
speaking purposes.

Organizations regularly promote people into leadership
roles because of their mastery or "intelligence" in their field. In
healthcare, a common practice is to promote the best clini-
cians into leadership roles due to their mastery of their technical craft. Strong logic guides this action; however, it has been
well documented that there are serious shortfalls when relying
on technical prowess alone to predict leadership success. It
turns out that leadership success has more factors determining
success than just technical know-how.

Basic "table stakes" for a leader include above-average ability to reason logically and process data, the ability to relate

effectively with others, a good sense of self, and effective communication skills – both oral and written.

However, another key attribute of leadership intelligence missing from these lists is a strong sense of inquisitiveness. The best leaders we have seen in organizations are inquisitive themselves and foster that spirit of inquiry in their organizations.

A good leader isn't the one with all the answers – a good leader is the one with the best questions. An inquisitive leader is almost by definition intellectually humble. Through their very questioning, leaders have to be aware of, and admit to, not knowing all the answers.

Some leaders who have this inquisitive intelligence may have it innately, but more likely it was developed over periods of formal education as well as their multiple life lessons. Similarly, organizations can be "taught" inquisitive intelligence.

In fact, there are whole methods and techniques taught by consulting companies to teach inquiry methodology. Names that may be familiar to the reader include Root Cause Analysis, the 5 Whys of Lean, Agile improvement, Continuous Process improvement, Toyota Production System, and many more. At the heart of each of these methods is the process of asking "why?" at least 5 times to get at the foundation (root cause) of a problem or issue that needs solving. In effect, this means using a structured drill down to root out the primary cause.

We've had personal experiences that underscore the challenges and difficulty of going through root cause analysis using 5 Whys. It can be tedious and frustrating and at times it feels to many as if they are making up answers just to complete the exercise. More often, when an organization drills down to the root of a problem, it can expose issues that are uncomfortable to address organizationally. It may expose underfunding of new product development, or a design error that was missed in production, or processes that were ignored during implementation. An organization, like the leader, needs the intellectual humility to admit errors and commit to fixing them. Persistence is helpful!

An organization that has inquisitive intelligence has leadership that embraces and models it. How do leaders foster inquisitive intelligence in themselves and in their organizations?

A leader developing inquisitive intelligence is intellectually restless – appreciating the great work of their organization but never fully satisfied with it.

The leader will search for ways to improve, comparing the organization's performance to competitors, regular benchmarking within and outside their industry.

The inquisitive leader also develops durable processes in the organization to assure that the organization continuously improves through a spirit of inquiry. These processes can include regular training in root cause (5 Whys) methods.

Results from this inquiry are frequently communicated in the organization including outputs from the use of these methods and how the organization improved as a result – celebrating these successes.

In short, inquisitiveness may prove to be the most important supporting link that ties intelligence to desired leadership-driven results.

Personal Leadership Questions (Intelligent)

- Am I open to new ideas and solutions and learning?
- How do I model a spirit of inquiry among those I lead?

Institutional Leadership Questions (Intelligent)

- How are good ideas rewarded in my organization?
- How is failure handled?

> The best leaders we know have coupled their strong intellectual skills with a spirit of inquiry that drives them to continued improvement and success.

Attribute 7: Resilience

Man plans ... God Laughs

– Old Yiddish Proverb

An element that is resilient has the capability to recover its size and shape after being deformed, especially by compressive stress. In engineering and other building trades, use of materials that are resilient and can withstand compressive forces such as hurricanes and earthquakes are studied and used to make buildings, bridges, and other infrastructure safer and more durable.

The application of the term resilience to the field of organizational management has been well researched and documented. There are all manner of lists and enumeration of characteristics, traits, and categories of resilient organizations and leaders – some of which are actually useful.

Why does it seem there is so much being written and discussed about resilience in the management literature?

A key reason is the sheer volume and rate of change that organizations and their leaders are facing – nothing like we have experienced before. It seems to us beyond debate that the adoption of digital technology is catalyzing the rates of change at an exponential rate across every category of industry and business. Daily we experience or read about this disruption, and change in how we shop, how we consume our news, and how we access new technologies. We are hard-pressed to think of any aspect of our lives untouched by this phenomenon.

Examples abound of organizations that failed to understand changes occurring in their industry and what they might mean in their organization...and thus are no longer in business. There are many reasons why this happened, but fundamentally they were not able to adapt and pivot to what the market was requiring of them to remain relevant. In terms of our definition at the start of this essay, these organizations were stressed by an external force and were unable to recover their size and shape after being deformed.

From our experience, organizational resilience isn't any one thing. It isn't just intelligence or discipline or effective communications, rather it is the synthesis of all the key leadership traits we have described in this book.

How do you know if your organization is resilient and how can you continue to develop that capability?

A resilient organization continuously monitors the market and is honestly assessing the impact of environmental developments on their business. A legitimate lesson has as its core the question, "How many companies have gone out of business thinking that Amazon was just a niche bookseller that couldn't possibly threaten their business?" A resilient organization cannot underestimate disruptive forces in its industry or in industries adjacent to it.

Resilient organizations make realistic plans and are fanatical about executing on those plans, and if a plan fails or needs to be adjusted, that adjustment is made in a timely manner. Many management teams in similar industries are often trying basically the same things to be successful. In our view, the differentiating factor of the successful teams is their ability to execute.

Management teams that are resilient have a certain emotional maturity about them. They are confident that they can be successful, but more than that, under pressure they manage their feelings and impulses so that they stay focused on the external threat and not break down into bickering and fighting among themselves. That's not to say there aren't strong exchanges of differing perspectives, but not so much as to destroy the functioning of the team and response to the external threat.

Resilient organizations have a well-developed ability to communicate among themselves but also to their teams and other external constituencies. Earlier we described the CEO as the "chief sense maker" in the organization. In a period of dramatic change and disruption, organizational threats occur more rapidly, and the organization must synthesize the meaning of that threat and how they will respond faster than ever before. A well-developed ability to communicate internally and externally the organization's response and direction in the face of those threats is critical to ongoing organization success.

Organizations, since they are made up of people, are living, breathing organisms. As such, they can learn, change, evolve, and adapt to the environment. To the degree they can learn to be resilient and recover their size and shape after being deformed by a compressive stress, they increase the likelihood that they will survive and succeed in the future.

And just as an organization needs to learn to be resilient, individuals need to as well. No one gets through their own career without some kind of "compressive force" hitting them: It is just the human condition.

Throughout your career, you will have experiences such as the death of a loved one, divorce, abrupt and unplanned job changes, personal health challenges – you get the idea. Yet it seems we approach our careers as if none of this will happen, so we fail to plan for when something inevitably does go horribly wrong.

The steps to maintaining individual resilience are essentially the same as those applied in an organization:

■ Continuous self-assessment and monitoring of personal relationships and your own well-being
■ Having a contingency plan for when things go "off the rails"
■ Keeping your head about you when things go wrong – reminding yourself that the bad times – just like the good times – don't last forever

■ Communicating with those close to you: Your family, a trusted colleague, a mentor, or a coach

A resilient leader will not get stuck on an "excuses escalator," nor waste too much time looking in the rear-view mirror: It will be time to recover, re-plan, and move forward with alacrity. If you and where you "hang your hat" are not leading toward the next phase, you are already too late!

Personal Leadership Questions (Resilience)

■ Are you the same person you were three years ago?
■ What has changed?
■ What should change?

Institutional Leadership Questions (Resilience)

■ How does your organization respond to crises?
■ What is the most momentous challenge in your industry?
■ How is your organization preparing for this challenge?

> Obsolescence may be delayed, but it is an unwavering result of any static plan. Change is a hallmark of successful human and organizational existence. Innovation drives; resilience pairs with innovation for successful rebounds from unpredictable and inevitable failures. Beware the perfect: It is the enemy of the good.

AND NOW WHAT? 2

> Truly successful decision making relies on a balance
> between deliberate and instinctive thinking
>   – Malcolm Gladwell

The vignettes that we've recounted are sometimes amusing, frequently horrifying, and always unfortunate, perhaps even tragic,
for the organizations served. The tragedy extends to the careers
and lives of the leaders and their colleagues for the majority
are Career Ending Opportunities (CEOs, the pundit replies). So
now that we have been amused and hopefully informed about
the travails of failed leadership episodes and the attributes that
predicate leadership: NOW WHAT? Are there predictive lessons
to be extracted and preventative strategies to be applied?

The answer is "YES," but work is involved. Though chance
is said to favor the prepared mind, there is always something
you can do to increase the favorable chances. Reading the
travails of leadership failure begins to increase the odds of
success by providing the "I would never be that stupid, craven,
foolish, or manipulated" reaction. But is that a realistic conclusion? Have you never erred out of sloth, knowledge deficit,
temptation? Has your career – or life for that matter – been
totally without a misstep? If your career has been blemish,

DOI: 10.4324/9781003304371-5

error, and doubt-free, something is amiss. Either you are not in touch with the reality of your situation or you've been playing it safe and not taking even calculated risks to grow, change, and advance. It may be time for a candid conversation with a career mentor, coach, or close professional friend if you really want to be on the path to growth as a leader.

Although the vignettes seem impossible at times, each and every one is real and representative of the errors and missed opportunity that is rampant in organizational leadership today, everywhere. These are not idiosyncratic, but in reality, are all too often characteristic of the people who have ascended to these roles.

Most of these failures represent the real-life implementation of the slippery slope phenomenon. The subject leaders didn't awake one day and declare, "I think I'll become a totally self-centered egotist and manipulate those around me." Nor did their epiphany include, "Gosh, I've decided to exhibit behavior that is so totally inappropriate to the organizational culture that I'll get terminated." Or, "Perhaps I'll display the temper management of a two-year-old and terrorize my subordinates." Few if any of the subject-failed leaders were conscious of their exhibited maladaptive behaviors, nor did many willingly select their choices as style options; yet, all failed their organizations and imperiled their careers.

Thoughtful planning for organizational succession is a tool to begin to use as soon as a leader becomes a leader. And as a leader, a significant trait to avoid is missing the element of personal growth – if for nothing else, then as a model for others to follow. Better yet, actually and intentionally "doing it."

Those two elements – planning and growing – lead inexorably toward constructive reframing for personal career and for the organization.

Thus, we'll tie the loose ends of this book together by following three threads: Organizational succession, personal growth, alternative framing; and then, a final admonition: Success builds on external experiences and personal failures!

Chapter 3

Planning for Orderly Organizational Succession

First, successful leaders plan for a self-replacement – whether at a known exit such as retirement or at a precipitous event such as illness. Leaders who are indispensable to the organization – that is, they can't possibly be replaced – can *not* be effective leaders. Indispensable leaders are not good leaders: They more likely are autocrats, egotists, or others who fit some even less desirable descriptors. Making oneself irreplaceable is the height of irresponsibility, failing the organization in a most elemental manner.

Leaders build resilient organizations with inherent capabilities able to assure that the organization continues to fulfill its mission. Much like Jim Collins' "flywheel" concept, organizations of any worth should be able to continue during even a disruptive or tragic transition.

DOI: 10.4324/9781003304371-6

A few examples of impediments to this goal follow.

1. Night of the living dead transition: Here, we witness an effective and beloved leader of many years standing prepare for retirement. The organization's Board completes a thorough and effective executive search and selects a promising candidate. The departing CEO helpfully suggests that he be retained to assist the new incumbent with onboarding. A grateful Board agrees, without consultation with the incoming heir. An overlap of tenure occurs resulting in months of a duopoly of sorts. The new CEO asserts his role and tries to implement what he sees as necessary changes. Staff subvert unwanted change by continuously looping the retiring CEO into their objections creating stress, tension, and inevitably a duel for organizational leadership. The Board gets pulled into the situation and the new leader is effectively undermined and departs, career in tatters. The retiring CEO returns to the formal post, though clearly he never really departed, and the search process begins again.

2. Gone but not forgotten: The retiring CEO is perceived as the genius who led the organization to the pinnacle. The Board recruits a new CEO but asks the retiring CEO to join the Board to assure continuity and continued success. The new replacement is cowed, intimidated, and effectively prevented from assuming the actual leadership role, because any substantive change will require the blessing of the previous leader. The organization muddles through an increasingly mediocre performance because change and evolution are eschewed out of fear of endangering the legacy of the past when that past has tremendous influence over the present through Board oversight.

3. The ghost of Christmas past: The CEO has built an organization dependent on her talents in relationships, marketing, and sales. Transferring these intangible but

marketable relationships to new leaders proves a monumental challenge. The new organizational leader responds by recruiting and beefing up traditional sales teams and strategies. The rapid transfer of leadership doesn't permit effective continuation of previous relationships and significant chunks of business are lost.

4. Beyond the "sell by" date: The CEO was a key factor in building an effective and efficient organization. His resolve, vision, and ability to recruit and retain great team members have resulted in a well-running company. But time and tide wait for no man and the CEO like all humans, ages. Increasingly "stuck in the way we've always done things," the organization begins to miss market and product innovation opportunities. The long-loved CEO works harder.

Succession is but one of the changes that are required if organizations are to survive, much less thrive. Combining and extending from some conclusions based on the trail-blazing research of Everett Rogers and quite separately of Charles Handy, we can note that there are useful cycles of innovation and significant timing to them.* The earlier the changes are made, the more effective they will be – assuming they are the correct changes to begin with!

If initiated when the idea, organization, or person has arrived is at the top of "the game," new ideas and changes tend to lead to stability for a time, though less to longer-term growth. Watch how the entities listed at the top of the DJIA change over time!

If held off until a decline has started, the competition will jump ahead and be very hard to catch.

With this in mind, let's now go to the second path.

---

* Both Handy and Rogers wrote numerous works relevant to this section beyond those cited in the bibliography.

Chapter 4

Modeling Career Growth as a Part of Succession

So how do you lower the odds of committing the big blunder? One trite but true saying, "Know thyself," holds the key. Brutally understanding your strengths, weaknesses, opportunities, and threats is a critical but potentially elusive accomplishment. Yes, this is the famous SWOT analysis turned inward. Although sounding complex at first blush, it can be an informal exercise that helps you prepare to seek the right role and avoid career mayhem.

A brief hour spent with pen and paper can render insights that provide directional information. Take the time to attain a quiet, reflective mood in a private space and relax and focus. A bit of deep breathing may help. Following is the mental exercise.

1. *Strengths*: Recall great accomplishments. What skills, attributes, and advantages do you possess that contributed to the outcome? Make a brief listing of same. Are you quick on your feet under stress? Contemplative and creative? Persistent and disciplined? Go ahead, brag to yourself a

DOI: 10.4324/9781003304371-7

bit and bask in the glow of knowing what you do well. These are your career strengths.

2. *Weaknesses*: Now comes a less fun, but perhaps more significant reflection. When have you performed poorly? Under great stress? Peer pressure? Temptation? Simply not well prepared for the task at hand? Wallow in reflection on your failures, there is great insight not only on career future but also direction on developmental goals and activities.

3. *Opportunities*: Cast your mind toward where you are and where you'd like to be. What opening in the future sets you on this path? Are there routes to your goal that might be obscure now, but could be revealed through scrutiny? Who, what, and where do you need to focus next to progress toward your goal?

4. *Threats*: These are tough to perceive, but what are the obstacles to getting where you aim? Are there barriers you can surmount by applying effort and attention? For example, are you not academically qualified for the role sought? If not, then devise a plan to address this shortfall and get going. Or are you geographically restricted and unable to move for the right opportunity? Are your financial constraints threatening to the point that any career move would be too risky or destabilizing to self and family? Be brutally candid and realistic. These threats represent the barriers to advancement and also, in some respects, a "To Do" list; what can you eliminate, change, modify? Which barriers must you learn to accept and work with?

Of course, the SWOT exercise above is just a back-of-the-envelope calculation: A quick and dirty first step to assuring that you don't appear in someone else's version of spectacular leadership failures. An additional good guide to developing as a leader is Blanchard and Miller's *Great Leaders*

Grow, particularly the Personal Assessment pages on 114–115, another useful exercise and guide for developing your innate leadership capability. Then look at the next page!

Now the quote from Blanchard and Miller that really applies: "In case you were wondering, there is no value in the assessment you just completed – the value lies in what you do next." In other words, much of what happens is outside of your control, but not all! You can manage the circumstances a bit by choosing to manage yourself even if others, chance, and fate don't always trend your way.

Another key to avoiding the catastrophe of leadership that many experience is successfully choosing, if possible, your next boss. By knowing yourself, your strengths, weaknesses, opportunities, and threats, you'll have a crude guide to understanding the attributes and characteristics you'll require in the next job to facilitate growth, advancement, and the accumulation of the experience needed to progress along your chosen career path.

Though we are employed by a company, most of us work for the manager who supervises us. The most enlightened, profitable, leading-edge companies have a few dunderheaded bosses whose staffs and employees rarely progress. The institution or company is important, but your boss is the critical factor in building a successful leadership career. A negative, controlling, or demanding boss can make life miserable: A workplace that suffocates and impedes advancement or any sense of satisfaction even in the most enlightened company.

If you're working for a maladapted boss: Start plotting your exit in the most expeditious fashion possible. If you're looking for the next opportunity: Evaluate your potential leader closely. Does her/his style resonate with yours? Is s/he trustworthy? Competent? Representative of the values and ideals you believe critical to effective management? If not, run, don't walk to the exits.

Chapter 5

Reframing for the Future

A few standout thoughts that bear to be noted here, and as a final preamble to reframing: Please consider these pages and your reactions to them as being food for thought (reflections), rather than prescriptions!

- Leadership that enhances successes after failures recognizes the importance of trusted advisors, mentors, and the ability to mentor others.
- Further underscoring a transition from a failure to success is a recognition of incoming and outgoing informal, as well as formal, leadership and leadership roles to support others and to be supported.
- As a matter of self-reflection, be aware that doing a few things well often is more important than much noisy unproductive motion.
- Also, as you try to copy or model what you may have read and liked in this book, do understand that an anecdotal approach, not a deep research approach, was what we thought might be most helpful to readers; there are other critics – such as some on your Board or other

DOI: 10.4324/9781003304371-8

governing bodies – who may be insistent on seeing underlying hard research data to support your justifications for intended changes.

So, to help reframe the environment for your possible usefulness, we conclude with two thoughts: (1) Said multiple times – fail to succeed; and, (2) our experience has shown that climbing out of our usual environment often is a good way to reframe for future success, hence the following paragraphs that grow out of the literature of ecology.

Finally, our wrap-up thoughts. Although it has been decades since Barry Commoner first posed the four laws of ecology, they still apply and aptly represent the rules that govern organizational life. Here's our interpretation and application to organizations:

1. *There is no away*: Organizations and people think they can shed staff, employees, business lines, and history, but there really is no escape from any of these. If you terminate the meanest person on your staff, it is like firing Jack the Ripper: Subordinates will say you got rid of the only person who was good with a knife! This doesn't mean that you shouldn't rid yourself of poor performers, bad business lines, or move to new horizons; just remember that everything is still findable, traceable, and impactful, but still make decisions on the totality of the facts before you.

2. *Everything is connected to everything else*: When you slap the side of a bowl of Jell-O, the whole contents reverberate. Similarly with any organization, change offices, move staff to new roles, launch a marketing campaign. Sure. Just understand that the impact of change extends far beyond the focus of the change.

3. *There ain't no such thing as a free lunch (TANSTAAFL).* Every move, decision, or change has a price, but it might not be immediately apparent. Unintended consequences occur with almost every major decision, and trying to model or game out the impact of decisions can lessen the impact of unintended consequences; but rest assured, everything has a cost or exacts a price. This doesn't mean avoid change, just understand that it comes with a price and be willing to pay.

4. *Mother Nature Knows Best:* The simpler and more natural the form, the more functional and efficient the outcome. Elaborate systems built to impress rarely deliver; complex rules and regulations are hard to enforce and rarely deliver the intended consequence. Occam's razor should be a handy implement for your organizational leadership toolbox.

So, succession becomes as much a conclusion as it is an implicit goal about "nexts" throughout the text.

Chapter 6

The Final Admonition

Fail to succeed!

This is not a conclusion that one cannot succeed as a leader. Rather, it is a reminder that failure is a lesson from which leadership can emerge. We believe that successful leadership is built upon lessons that must grow out of leadership failures observed and experienced.

In short: Fear not failing. Fear only not learning from it. Perhaps better said: "Fail in Order to Succeed."

Lincoln may have said it even better: "My great concern is not whether you have failed, but whether you are content with your failure."

We say: "Fail. Fix it. Move on!"

The issue with leadership here is whether there is intestinal fortitude and patience to focus on institutional (and career) mission and priorities. The attributes we've discussed can get you there.

It has been our pleasure to share the tales of leaders and failures. Recall that a failed strategy, job, or decision doesn't mean a failed leader. "No mistakes" indicates no risk and a stagnant life. But use this book to enlighten and avoid the

DOI: 10.4324/9781003304371-9

most obvious of errors. Our wish is that you contribute to your organization, professional life, and career by making new, innovative mistakes and learn from them!

> Know when to hold 'em, and when to fold 'em
> – Wisdom from the game of poker

Appendix:
Tracking Matrix

> Be yourself, because everyone else is taken
>   – Oscar Wilde

It is rare for a single point of failure to bring down an organization or its leader(s). In the section following this, vignettes are categorized against the leadership qualities defined above. The selections are somewhat arbitrarily assigned to help a reader self-identify for the purpose of heading off a failure or being able to a remedy.

While the literature is rich in leadership approaches, many miss focusing on an important ingredient: absent some failures along the way, very few are able to be successful in significant leadership roles. It is a story that many are reluctant to share, but so very clearly has contributed to later successes.

Attitude combines with the fabled "10,000 hours of practice" to make it seem easy, particularly when some of those early "hours" have included mopping-up endeavors after your messes.

The table following is included as a possible helpful tool as you (re-)evaluate your "do-it-yourself" assessments. Mark up in any way that could help you see where your fit is within your organization and your alignment of current behaviors and practices and where you might want to be some time down the road.

Tracking Matrix Table

Vignette Working Title	V#	Integrity	Aware	Mature	Communication	Decisive	Intelligent	Resilient
Well-prepared for the Wrong Role	1							
Counter-cultural Leadership	2							
Well Qualified, But Lazy	3							
Sick Organization Syndrome (SOS)	4							
Large and In Charge	5							
Weak Moral Compass	6							
You Can Stay Too Long	7							
Symbols and Behaviors Communicate More Than Words	8							
A Single Source of Truth Needs to be Verified	9							
Temper Tantrums Are for Two-Year Olds	10							
Rip Off the Bandage	11							
Keep the Personal Away from the Professional	12							
Leader's Mind, But Not Brain, Is Lost	13							

(Continued)

(Continued)

Tracking Matrix Table		Integrity	Aware	Mature	Communication	Decisive	Intelligent	Resilient
Vignette Working Title	*V#*							
Family Business or Business of the Family?	14							
Bureaucratic Success, Mission Leadership Failure	15							
Leadership Failure Cascade	16							
Boards Bruise the Business	17							
Activity Is Not Productivity	18							
Small Intervention but Huge Impact	19							
No-Bell Prize	20							

Annotated References

Clearly, this is not intended as an academic masterpiece. Rather, we hope it will serve as a guideline for improvement via not so much a paradigm or "initiative-driven" template, but rather several stories that mirror experiences that may have started out very badly, but also which have left behind a trail of options to think about in your own leadership path.

A few older works are mingled with a sampling of more recent writings that may impart some profound "think-abouts" for your idle or pressured consideration. Several stories are ideal for graduate discussions – be they in healthcare, business, politics, science, or wherever!

- **Blanchard, Kenneth**, 1982, *The One Minute Manager*, William Morrow and Co. (New York)

  Popular reading for "wannabe managers on their way up." Many editions and subsequent products by this motivational speaker and colleagues. Focus is on effective leadership for different kinds of people: adaptive styles for various situations.

- **Blanchard, Ken**, and **Mark Miller**, 2012, *Great Leaders Grow*, Berrett-Kohler Publishers (San Francisco, CA)

A combination of storytelling and cheer-leading, this small book focuses on multiple ways to focus readers on continuing growth and self-assessments, then pushes the reader toward the all-important "next" activity for continued growth.

- **Block, Peter, et al.**, 2011, *Flawless Consulting: A Guide to Getting Your Expertise Used,* John Wiley & Sons (New York)
- **Block, Peter**, 2013, (2nd ed.), *Stewardship: Choosing Service Over Self-Interest,* John Wiley & Sons (New York)

Both Block books are among his many acclaimed writings on leadership, business, and organizational design: focusing on the wider good for the larger especially in our growing dependence on a virtual world.

- **Bolles, Richard N.**, 2021, *What Color Is Your Parachute?,* Ten Speed Press (Berkeley)

For over 50 years of almost annual updates, a premier source for job-seekers' self-assessment tools useful for many rethinking career options.

- **Brooks, Arthur C.**, 2019, "Your Professional Decline Is Coming (Much) Sooner Than You Think," *The Atlantic (July):* https://www.theatlantic.com/magazine/archive/2019/07/work-peak-professional-decline/590650/

Brooks, a former CEO of the American Enterprise Institute, and Professor of Practice of Public Leadership at Harvard Kennedy School concludes that your work peak is earlier than you think.

- **Brown, Brené**, 2018, *Dare to Lead: Brave Work. Tough Questions. Whole Hearts,* Random House (New York)

She emphasizes the need for courage and curiosity as integral to organizational leadership. Related to Brown's popular TED talk, and selected by Bloomberg as a book of the year, Dare is an instructive, insight-filled text for all current and aspiring organizational leaders.

■ **Caslen, Jr., Robert L.,** and **Michael D. Matthews**, 2020, *The Character Edge*, St. Martin's Press (New York)

A treatise on how to build character-based leadership, numerous examples of character's impact on leadership and the essential elements of character.

■ **Collins, James C.**, 2001, *Good to Great,* Harper Collins (New York)

An in-depth analysis of the attributes that separate good companies from great companies, including a focus on recruiting and retaining great people and the elusive "fly wheel" concept.

■ **Collins, Jim**, 2009, *How the Mighty Fall – And Why Some Companies Never Give In*, Harper Collins (New York)

The author outlines the stages of organizational decline, emphasizes the role of hubris in same, and notes strategies for preventing or remedying decline for leaders.

■ **Commoner, Barry**, 1971, *The Closing Circle*, Alfred A. Knopf (New York)

Barry Commoner was the driving force behind recognition of the four informal laws of ecology and a founding thought leader of the environmental movement.

■ **Covey, Stephen R.**, 2020, *The 7 Habits of Highly Effective People: 30th Anniversary Edition*, Simon & Schuster (New York)

Another book with millions of copies in print that has impacted untold numbers of readers and leaders in many fields.

■ **Diamandis, Peter H.**, and **Steven Kotler**, 2020, *The Future is Faster Than You Think: How Converging Technologies are Transforming Business, Industries, and Our Lives*, Simon & Schuster (New York)

A follow-up to earlier writings dealing with large global issues, such as energy and hunger, this book makes predictions about the path of technologies that have created entrepreneurial responses to emerging and disruptive technologies affecting transportation, retail, advertising, education, health, entertainment, food, and finance.

■ **Deming, W. Edwards,** 2012, *The Essential Deming: Leadership Principles from the Father of Quality*, McGraw Hill (New York)

The founder of the quality movement has impacted every industry. This text condenses his thoughts and gives the reader a taste of the principles of TQM (Total Quality Management).

■ **Edmondson, Amy C.**, 2011, "Strategies for Learning from Failures," *Harvard Business Review,* 89(4) 48–55, 137

Includes a useful typology, "A spectrum of reasons for failing," ranging from blameworthy to praiseworthy, in support of her notion that "not all failures are created equally," leading to categorizing failures into three broad categories: preventative, complexity-related, and intelligent. A reader's challenge might be to find parallels for her organizational focus to individual leadership failures.

■ **Epstein, David**, 2019, *Range: Why Generalists Triumph in a Specialized World,* Riverhead Books (New York)

Stories illustrate the view that early-in-life specialization is an exception for later excellence, and that early failures lead to learning and fulfillment. The implication for leadership is reflected in our book.

■ **Erikson, Thomas**, 2017, *Surrounded by Psychopaths*, St. Martin's Press (New York)

Erikson gives solid advice for coping effectively with psychopaths in daily life, how to recognize their manipulative behaviors, and how to manage your own behavior for maximum protection.

■ **Fenner, K.**, 2009, "Hospital Near-Death Experience – How Medicare Termination Can Push Your Hospital to the Brink of Closing," *Originally a Guide Published for Clients:* http://www.compass-clinical.com/wp-content/uploads/2009/08/Hospitals-Near-Death-Full.pdf

Based on a real case history a telling of a significant "save," bringing an essential regional hospital back to life—and in record time—through smart and attentive leadership.

■ **Grant, Adam**, 2021, *Think Again*, Viking (New York)

New and popular approach to rethinking our imbedded models for thinking. Grant's lively style and clear logic gives great food for thought.

■ **Handy, Charles**, 1990, *The Age of Unreason*, Harvard Business School Press (Boston, MA)
■ **Handy, Charles**, 1994, *The Age of Paradox*, Harvard Business School Press (Boston, MA)

These are two of the classic works by an organizational thinker beyond compare. He forces a reader to consider alternate ways to rethink working business and life assumptions. At the least, a reader must recognize how what "was" may no longer "be."

■ **Hill, Linda A.**, and **Lineback, Kent**, 2019, *Being the Boss*, HBR Press (Brighton, MA)

The responsibilities and obligations of being in charge are explored and codified. Particularly useful for newly promoted "bosses" needing guidance and reassurance.

■ **Holt, Jim**, 2018a, "Overconfidence and the Monty Hall Problem," in *When Einstein Walked with Gödel*, p. 289–291, Farrar, Straus and Giroux (New York)
■ **Holt, Jim**, 2018b, "Say Anything," in *When Einstein Walked with Gödel*, p. 333–344, Farrar, Straus and Giroux (New York)

Holt differentiates "bullshit" from lying and gives ample examples of each in action. He also empathizes more with liars because they have moral clarity about what they are saying.

■ **Konnikova, Maria**, 2020, *The Biggest Bluff: How I Learned to Pay Attention, Master Myself, and Win*, Penguin Books (New York)

While the topic is the game of poker, the book really is about the psychology of winning, and a relevant special focus goes beyond strategy, with a strong emphasis on "The Art of Losing." Think risk-aversiveness vs. graceful resilience! It is an easy jump to understanding not only how to know one's adversaries (competitors), but also oneself and how to gauge and apply probabilities of success to necessary negotiations.

▪ **Korzybski, Alfred**, 1933 (and various editions and excerpts), *Science and Sanity,* available editions published by the Society of General Semantics (Ft. Worth, TX, but now headquartered in Forest Hills, NY).

First written in response to Hitler's lead-in to WW2, he lays out the basis for later writings in General Semantics. Included in this listing as a reminder that "The map is not the territory." Leaders' readings or generation of labels does not "make it so."

▪ **Kotler, Steven**, 2021, *The Art of Impossible*, Harper Collins (New York)

American author with articles in over 70 publications, he has focused his writings on ultimate human performance.

▪ **Kotter, John**, 2012, *Leading Change*, HBR Press (Brighton, MA)

Kotter's seminal work describing change not as an exception, but as an ongoing and ever-present process. He details an 8-step process for effectively managing change.

▪ **Kruse, Kevin**, 2019, *Great Leaders Have No Rules*, Rodale (Emmaus, PA)

Kruse presents a contrarian perspective on traditional leadership principles, positing and poking many accepted tropes to suggest an alternative approach.

◼ **Maister, David, et al.**, 2001, *The Trusted Advisor,* Touchstone (now via Simon & Schuster, New York)

They argue that technical mastery of discipline is insufficient. Trust and confidence must be earned, which they demonstrate through anecdotes. Later editions with changing supporting or lead authors include updated commentaries and toolkits that many find useful in their endeavors.

◼ **McHarg, Ian L.**, 1991, *Design With Nature*, John Wiley & Sons (New York)

A beautiful example of breaking out of a disciplinary silo to demonstrate far-reaching leadership (in urban/regional planning). Lewis Mumford wrote of this work: "In presenting us with a vision of organic exuberance and human delight, which ecology and ecological design promise to open up for us, McHarg revives the hope for a better world."

◼ **McKeown, Greg**, 2020 (Paperback version), *Essentialism: The Disciplined Pursuit of Less,* Tim Dugan Books (Currency, RandomHouse/Penguin, New York)

A prescriptive game plan for getting (and giving) more out of life with a less-is-more (doing a few things very well beats doing many things but not so well) approach that is very applicable both to institutional leadership and personal careers.

◼ **Patton, Michael Quinn**, 2017, *Facilitating Evaluation, Principles in Practice,* Sage Publications (Thousand Oaks, CA)

Perhaps the pre-eminent text dealing with a subject all too often lost or ignored by uncertain leaders: how best to engage the evaluation process ... especially when major changes are being considered. Written by an author with decades of experience with several processes with a wide variety of clienteles, this work should help inform any leader about a necessary art.

■ **Perlroth, Nicole**, 2020, *This Is How They Tell Me the World Ends*, Bloomsbury Publishing (New York)

An ultimate telling of strategic and tactical wins, losses, recoveries, and restarts that point to leadership lessons, the importance of timing, listening, looking, and acting: its focus is on the cyber-weapons race, but the underlying theme could be titled "Leadership Failures 101."

■ **Peters, Thomas J.**, and **Waterman, Robert H.**, 2003 (and later editions). *In Search of Excellence*, Harper Business Essentials (New York)

A research-based well-known organizational study from which emerged eight widely-cited attributes characterizing excellent companies.

■ **Powell, Colin**, 1995, *My American Journey*, Random House (New York)

An autobiographical story demonstrating a leadership path that is the antithesis of the entitled expectation of too many who rise into leadership positions that fail because of the lack of work and commitment needed by "outsiders" to break into that atmospheric level.

■ **Rogers, Everett M.**, 1962, *Diffusion of Innovations*, Simon & Schuster (New York)

Through this and in later editions, "Ev," who coined the title term, explained how new ideas spread via communication channels over time, even when initially perceived as uncertain and even risky. His logistic curve demonstrates the rate of idea acceptance—really an "S-curve. Leaders should understand how it rails off with time.

■ **Rubenstein, David M.**, 2020, *How to Lead: Wisdom from the World's Greatest CEOs, Founders, and Game Changers,* Simon & Schuster (New York)

He interviewed visionaries, builders, transformers, commanders, decision makers, and masters. Like most recent authors in leadership literature, the focus was on positive characteristics (13 were targeted), not on the failure side of the coin or recovery from same. None-the-less, a useful contrasting perspective to ours, with convergent conclusions.

■ **Sandberg, Sheryl Kara**, 2013, *Lean In: Women, Work, and the Will to Lead,* Alfred A. Knopf (New York)

An American business executive, billionaire, and philanthropist outlines the barriers to leadership roles faced by women, and suggests strategies to confront each one. She provides a useful guide to women launching a career or facing mid-career challenges.

■ **Snyder, Timothy**, 2017, *On Tyranny: Twenty Lessons from the Twentieth Century,* Tim Dugan Books (Crown/ Penguin, New York)

Full of lessons broadly applicable to leadership when seeking to build and instill trust and integrity into an organization and eschew authoritarian dominance. (Also available in a very accessible and slightly updated 2021 graphic book version.)

Index

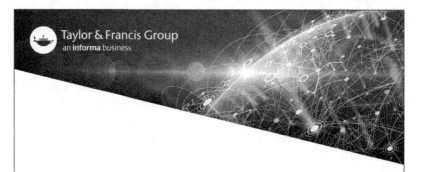

Printed in the United States
by Baker & Taylor Publisher Services